CW01643001

Deep in the Wealden forest lies the old manor house, Mantlemass, the one constant factor in an ever-changing world. The Mantlemass novels trace the shifting fortunes of a family through two turbulent centuries, showing how the lives of ordinary folk are touched by great events.

The Eldest Son is the story of Harry, eldest son of Medley and Catherine whose story was told in *The Sprig of Broom.*

Time and again, Harry's quick temper and impatience put him into conflict with his father and set him apart from his brothers, Piers and Richard. He has no interest in, or love for, the horses that the Medleys breed at Ghylls Hatch. The forest rings with the sound of iron foundries and Harry nurses a secret ambition to become an iron master, to conquer an element as fiery and unyielding as himself. Harry's other ambition, equally fervent, is to marry Anne, daughter of Sir John Furnival.

Time brings Harry success in his home life, but after years of constant wrangling with his father he is no nearer to his dream of establishing a foundry. Then Harry makes a serious mistake which threatens the whole way of life at Ghylls Hatch, and alters the course of his future.

Other Mantlemass novels published by Macdonald

The Lark and the Laurel
The Sprig of Broom
A Cold Wind Blowing

Forthcoming titles

The Iron Lily
A Flight of Swans
Harrow and Harvest
The Keys of Mantlemass
The Miller's Boy

The Eldest Son

BARBARA WILLARD

Macdonald

Illustrations by Alan Marks
Cover design by Jerry Watkiss
Book design by Ewing Paddock

A Macdonald Book

First published in Great Britain in 1977 by Penguin Books Ltd

This edition published in Great Britain in 1988 by
Macdonald & Co (Publishers) Ltd
London & Sydney

British Library Cataloguing in Publication Data

Willard, Barbara
The eldest son.—(Mantlemass series).
I. Title II. Series
823'.914[J] PZ7

ISBN 0-356-13174-2
ISBN 0-356-13175-0 Pbk

Typeset by Leaper & Gard Ltd, Bristol
Printed and bound in Great Britain by
Robert Hartnoll (1985) Ltd, Cornwall

Macdonald & Co (Publishers) Ltd
Greater London House
Hampstead Road
London NW1 7QX

A member of Maxwell Pergamon
Publishing Corporation plc

CONTENTS

1

Falcon

Once, when Harry Medley was eight or nine years old, his mother, rebuking him for some small offence, had called him her *young falcon*. 'For,' she had told him, 'you do ever hover above what you most desire. And though you might see it to be wrong, and know it to be so, and know you must wait to take it, yet you will have it — and like the falcon, swoop at last and carry it away.'

No one had been near at that time; none else had heard her admonition, for it was never repeated. It was between the two of them, as often things did seem to be. He was her firstborn, first pledge of the great love between herself and his father, and it was as if she could not forget it. She would set father and son side by side to match likenesses; and though soon she had two sons, and was easy and merry with both, yet she never quite concealed that she favoured the first. So that when she called him *falcon*, even in admonishment, he was proud of her words and knew them to be true – whatever the enterprise he would indeed hover and watch, with difficulty maintaining patience, and then at the best moment, strike. As he grew older this was more and more apparent. His mother was no longer there to nod and say, 'It is as I supposed', and it might even be that because she was gone and deeply mourned he shaped himself to the pattern she had seen in him. Particularly this was so because he was often in conflict with his father, who seemed to him to favour the second son, Piers.

By the time he was eighteen years old, there were two things Harry Medley had marked for his own. Neither would be easy to attain. But in time he knew he would have both.

The youngest brother, Richard, was six that year. Piers, in the middle, coming up to fifteen. Between them had been three other sons, but none had lived, and when Richard was born their mother died. For the little boy, the sun rose and set with his brother Piers – yet it was dark-haired Harry he was most like in face and colour, and Harry who took very little notice of him. Therefore, when Harry did show some favour to Richard, he appeared to his younger brother as a compound of their father, of the King, of the Pope, and even – if this were not a shade blasphemous – of Our Blessed Lord. When Harry crooked a finger, Richard ran to obey in awe and flattery.

'Get Matthew or Rafe saddle up Argent,' Harry commanded Richard one warm spring afternoon. 'I'll ride you out, an hour or two hour.'

It did not occur to him that Richard might be engaged in some more demanding ploy, and he was right. Richard was hammering himself a cart to go on wheels and carry the kindling loads he was required to bring indoors each day – there was no single soul in that household who lived without his given task. His *bavins cart*, Richard called it, but he dropped it readily when Harry shouted his command.

'Where, then?' he asked, as they rode out side by side,

Richard on his pony, Argent, Harry as usual on a horse too big for him – not because he was such a brilliant horseman, but because he was not very tall and enjoyed the feeling of power and authority given by a big mount.

'One way, t'other way,' was all he replied to Richard's query.

He rode on ahead knowing that Richard followed obediently, on the long track that soon left Ghylls Hatch, their home, well behind them. From its sprawl of buildings, none very grand, though there had been some domestic building ten years or so ago, they came then within sight of Mantlemass, where their grandmother, Dame Cecily Mallory, lived with her eldest son and his family. But Harry turned aside before reaching the Mantlemass boundary, and shifted across the river by way of the ford, and then uphill again, over the far long bank, beyond and behind the great beech hanger that held the heights to the north-west, and so came at last within sight of the forest pale. There the spire of Staglye church seemed to touch the eastward sky, pale and high in the light spring sunshine. Turning yet again, and shifting downhill, they came to where a spread of water lay below them, with beyond it a scatter of buildings and over all a huge noise and smoke, and a shouting of men about some great heavy work. The leaves of tender green, the spreading fingers of the great birches, the hint of gold along the branches of the more reluctant oak, the lingering primroses, all showed in their frailty an almost grotesque contrast to what went on below and around.

Harry had been from the first set towards this destination, but as they reached it he was aware that Richard was hanging behind.

'Did you ever pass this way, Dickory?'

'Aye. Once I did.'

Harry saw with surprise that the boy was frightened. 'Well, then – what troubles you?'

'I saw a dread thing,' said Richard.

There was an iron foundry here. Richard had taken out Argent and ridden with wild and forbidden boldness far from home. He had chanced by this place at the very instant when there had been an overspill of molten metal and two men had been caught by it. One was slightly burned, the other fatally. The whole fury and frenzy of the place, its hellish dark and fire, had been made even more hideous to the child by the terrible shouting screams of the victim's mortal anguish. When at last he died, the silence that settled seemed the death of more than one man. The whole forest stood back and no one among those watching spoke for what seemed many minutes. Then one had said, 'God rest him. Send for his wife.' But she was already running towards the place from where she had been driving the pigs a quarter of a mile away, and the silence broke entirely as she began to shriek in her turn. After that, the pace of the furnace's toil was taken up quickly to make good lost time, and Richard had ridden for home as though pursued by devils . . .

'What dread thing?' asked Harry.

'I forget,' said Richard, looking sick and pale.

'But do you know, then, what I'm to show you?'

The boy nodded, but still hung back.

'Come now, leave Argent tethered wi' Dapple.' As Richard still hesitated, Harry said sharply, 'Come now, I say. Do's I bid, Dickory Medley!'

He watched Richard as he slid slowly from the saddle, and took long over fumbling a hitch to tether Argent. He hunched his shoulders in a manner Harry hated to see – this last of Catherine Medley's sons had a thick shoulder that he often tried to disguise by pulling up the other to match it, most of all when he was nervous or distressed. For a second Harry stood scowling at him, then his better nature took charge. He put a hand on his little brother's neck and pulled him and shoved him along, but in a friendly fashion.

'There's naun to fear,' he said.

'Shall it be running?' Richard asked. 'Shall they be running the iron, brother?'

'Aye, b' the sounds of it.'

'Then shan't it spatter us?'

'Why? Come we stand apart – and who's likely to let us do otherly?'

The clamour was growing as they came nearer, the thumping, clanging sound of the great hammer dominating all. This had been the first iron mill working near home to use water power to drive the hammer and work the great ox-hide bellows. The sound of water was almost as strong as the hammer's thud. Richard could tell that Harry was in a mood of high excitement, but he could not see why. Medleys lived by horses, so what could iron mean to Harry, eldest of the Medley sons and set towards a goodly inheritance?

The place greeted them not only with sound but with smell – of charcoal, of smoke; of roasting ore; of water hissing into vapour, of men in a high sweat. As Harry and Richard stepped clear of the trees that lined the track, children scattered like sparrows and fled silently towards the cluster of hovels on the higher bank. And at that, as at some arranged warning signal, a man came to the door of the one solid stone house in sight and stood looking across towards the brothers.

'That's the founder,' Harry told Richard. He called out, shouting against the clamour, 'I come again – like I say last time!'

The man did not shout back, but came from his house easily and slowly. Harry Medley might be the eldest son of a prospering neighbour with gentry connections, but iron bred a pride that was well able to discount such advantages. When he was within talking distance it was because Harry had seen fit to advance to meet him, as many such would not; and when he spoke it was only to say, 'Good day,' his voice rumbling from a huge chest, then husking over as it reached a throat scoured by smoke and heat.

'This time I brought my young brother,' Harry said. 'Richard – here's Gaffer John, who's master of all these works and the men that toil in 'em.'

'But not over cold iron, only the hot,' the man said, significantly grimacing. He meant that, since the forest was Crown land, and certain rights on certain grounds farmed out, the finished iron, be it ploughshare or bombard, belonged to his lordship who held these privileges from King Henry. Gaffer John, in spite of his huge chest, was shortish, and his skin had the hard dark appearance of over-tanned leather, or more nearly of his own roasted ore. His true name was Urry, and he was cousin to Urrys who had smelted ambitiously some years past, and then declined in business. Like his father before him, this Urry was called *Blackman*, and so his sons might well be called and the old name be forgotten.

He looked down at Richard, and Richard saw what he did not want to see and tried vainly to look away. Laughing, Gaffer John Blackman stooped until his face was level with Richard's. He pulled at the lower lid of his left eye, displaying an empty socket.

'There's none can master iron, hot or cold. See there. See what hot iron do – come a man treat it false and scambly.'

Richard shrank back against his brother, but Harry caught his arm and pulled him round, shaking him a bit, annoyed at his timidity. He hung on when Richard struggled and tried to sidle off.

'This is man's work I brought you to! Are you such a baby? Stand firm!'

The furnace, though not the largest about the forest, was a good deal bigger than most. There were many small hearths laid by men willing to take their advantage of the ore waiting to be dug, and to chance the penalties of being found out. Here at Blackman's the business was both more ordered and more impressive. The ponds were very big and just now carried a vast weight of water. The place now, with its founday, or term of work, running in the third or fourth day, gave a display of power that was frightening. Here man appeared to have conquered many elements – water, air and fire were harnessed to the iron worker's purposes. Here, indeed, man was master in a hell of his own devising, to which not only he was condemned but his sons and his grandsons down to unknown and unnumbered generations – or so it was bound to seem to Harry Medley, building his own imagined future.

The brothers followed the founder as he advanced towards the furnace without any question as to why Harry had come. The noise increased with every step. Blackman jerked his head at Richard and shouted close by Harry's ear, 'See her stand well back.' And then he grinned at Richard, and tapped his left eye socket in gruesome reminder.

'Let the boy be, gaffer,' Harry said then.

Richard slunk along, one hand clutching at Harry's belt, as if otherwise the clamour itself might trip him and then he must surely be consumed by smoke and fire. He walked with shut eyes, but kept opening them stealthily, then snapping them shut again – so that in a series of blurred and broken images he saw the furnacemen working to a rhythm he did not understand, whose power yet strongly caught at his imagination: the man stationed aloft to feed the furnace – his fellows coming and going, many of them near naked – the orders given and received by the scorched and sweating workers; then the shouts, the sudden dreadful hissing as the molten metal was tapped off and ran, liquid and perilous, from the hearth.

Between Harry and the gaffer a shouting talk was bandied, full of words strange to Richard but which Harry mouthed almost lovingly – shingling, looping; bloom, chafery, sow, pig, cinder; finery ... And always hammer, pond, spillway, leat, bay ... Harry spoke this language haltingly, as though he had learnt it in a dream. And in a dream he felt himself moving still. He put his arm suddenly round Richard's shoulders, glancing down at him with a strange, sharing expression, as if he would impose upon his young brother a magic from which he might never quite escape ...

It was dark by the time Harry was able to drag himself away. The excitement left him and he snapped at Richard to keep up and stop stumbling. The tethered horses were restive and stamping, greeting them loudly.

'Now watch where you ride,' Harry said, still sharp and admonishing. 'And sit up. You're all aslew.'

The boy was in fact worn out. They had ridden a fair way and then stood in the clamour of the iron-working for almost all the afternoon. Home seemed far away. Harry's great beast, however, was sure-footed, and Argent picked his way after with delicate precision. At last the dark overtook them and they dropped to a walk.

'Shall you ever be an ironfounder, brother?' Richard asked.

'Aye. Though none know it but you. Do you find that mad? Our father and Piers are bound to.'

'You never could do a mad foolish thing, Harry,' the child answered, humble and admiring. 'Never. Any know that.'

'It's the best new way to a fortune, Dickory, iron is.'

'Should you make ploughs, and crooks?'

'Guns and gunstones, more like. Any day, we'll be back fighting the French or the Scots – or some other such barbarians. Mine iron, you mine gold, surelye!'

They rode the last mile to a rising moon, and by then Harry saw uneasily that Richard was half out of his saddle, and yawning as he rode. Judith Springer, who kept house for them all at Ghylls Hatch, and had cared for Richard ever since his birth, would have some smart words to say about that. She cosseted the boy, Harry thought – but then he had taken the place of her own child. One way and another, the Medleys were much beholden to Judith. She had moved into the terrible gap left by their mother's death, without ever presuming to take her place . . .

'Where'd he take you?' she was asking Richard later, sitting by him and coaxing him to one more spoonful of groats, and then one more; she always feared for some weakness in his general health to match his shoulder. 'Clean the bowl. Good fare's never to be wasted. Eat up, child.' Then she asked again – 'Where did you ride with your brother?'

'Far away.'

'That's a fair word of Harry. He's for ever some way away, even come he's sitting by the fire wi' us. But this time it was far?'

He nodded, his mouth full. He would rather not speak of it, even to Judith, whom secretly he called mother.

'We'll lose him one day,' she was saying, half to herself. 'I pray it shall not kill your father.'

On Easter Sunday that same year, they rode to mass at Staglye church – the master, his sons, Judith; with eight at least of the servants, the women riding pillion. Whatever shirking of religious duties might leave the church a shade empty at other times, it was bound to be full at Easter. At that season a man might do his least duty and still assure himself he kept the favour of heaven. The village priest, truly, was harder to please, but then the souls of his parishioners were his purpose in life. And so he would hound them and plead with them and weep over them and for them; he was a good man, if difficult to please.

They rode by way of Mantlemass, and there extended the cavalcade. Dame Cecily rode out to join them, with Simon Mallory, her son, his wife, Mary, and their two elder daughters, Margaret and Elizabeth; the youngest, Susannah, was left at home – which disappointed Richard who was fond of her even though she was a year his junior. Six servants rode in attendance, the lesser sort having already tramped the miles there and back for mass near daybreak. The two parties greeted one another warmly but quietly, and then rode on in silence; their Easter rejoicings would begin after they had received the sacrament.

It was a little after eight o'clock, the morning misted but with a promise of later sunshine. There was promise, in fact, over everything. In this part of the forest the bluebells were already thick under the beech trees, and thrusting through the dry trusses of last year's bracken, pouring along the banks above ditches where channelled water ran fast and tinkling, washing the gnarled roots of huge and ancient trees. And over all, the confusion of birdsong, so netted and twisted in threads of varying sound that it was not possible to be sure which bird sang what song. Riding alongside his grandmother, Richard did try to sort one from the other. He frowned over it, and opened his mouth to share the puzzle with her – but looking down she smiled, and said, 'Say your prayers now. The rest shall wait.'

Rebuked, however kindly, Richard flushed. He was a little out of tune with such serious matters just lately. His one important prayer could never be answered, and he knew now that, short of a miracle, he had to put up with the thick shoulder he had prayed might be smoothed and straightened. He glanced back at his brothers, at Piers riding upright and forward in the newer style, at Harry using an old carved saddle with a high cantel. Harry, the boy decided, was another who was not saying his prayers. He was thinking perhaps, on such matters as iron . . .

And so he was, for it was in his mind constantly. He had sworn Richard to secrecy over their visit to the foundry; he need not have done, for Richard's instinct had instructed him. Harry had never learnt the patient love of horses that enslaved his father and his brother Piers. He looked upon them, truly, as a means to the livelihood of the Ghylls Hatch household. He admired the looks of them and the excitement of breaking and training, but he knew he could leave the daily trade in them and never miss it. 'Harry will break a horse,' his father had once said, 'but my young Piers will gentle it.' And this was so. Harry was too hot and hard, he matched his wits and his physical strength against the animal's, and for pride's sake could not go at it mildly. He mastered his horses, and they were obedient, but too soon – there was none of the strange love that existed between Piers and the creatures he had handled expertly and tenderly ever since he was ten years old. Their father was saddened by this, and Harry knew it well, and how hard a fight would be ahead when the moment came to press his own ambitions for a different trade.

Outside the church at Staglye village, a groom was standing with three riding horses, his own nag and a pack animal. He was a stranger, and so all eyes were aware of him, and when the church was entered, then every gaze sought the strangers he attended – a tall man, rather shabbily cloaked but with an air of dignity, with a young girl who was not much more than a child and beside her an old bundle of a woman who must be her nurse. Since the full congregation was made up of familiar faces, these three stood in a kind of isolation. When Master Medley walked down the nave, with his mother-in-law, Dame Cecily, on his arm, he paused and bowed to the stranger, and the stranger austerely returned the greeting.

'Harry,' said his father, 'go to them and beg them to worship here beside us.'

So Harry crossed the nave and saluted the stranger.

'Sir, my father, Master Medley of Ghylls Hatch, prays that you may hear mass beside him.'

'Thank him for his courtesy. I am Sir John Furnival, journeying from the west to my manor in Kent.'

He looked over to the cohort from Ghylls Hatch and Mantlemass. After a second's clear consideration, he allowed Harry to bow him to his new place; but he left his daughter, as she must surely be, and the nurse behind him. Harry was immediately aware of a certain free-and-easy country manner and practice in his own people, and felt a bumpkin. He had once spent half a year with a gentry relative of his grandmother's in London; but, at fifteen, courtly ways had not been at all to his taste; he had pestered and nagged to be brought home. Now he glanced uneasily at the Mantlemass and Ghylls Hatch people, all higgledy-piggledy in the church, young and old, man, woman and child, and even to a degree, servant and master, as the fancy took them – Dame Cecily's

companion, Jess Truley, comfortably at her side, and beyond her the manor reeve with his wife and daughter. Harry frowned and felt uneasy. What would Sir John Furnival think of such confusion? In spite of his shabby cloak, he was a man of great presence.

This all distracted Harry greatly, and though the rest clearly did well at their devotions, he was unable to submit his thoughts meekly. The final blessing came as a relief to him. He felt ashamed and penitent – hastily admitting his fault as he bowed his head.

Even so, it was difficult to keep his eyes closed, and a slight move across the nave instantly distracted him. He turned his bowed head slightly, looking over his hands – and found the young stranger at her nurse's side doing the same. She peered round the edge of her hood, her manner modest, pious – yet recognizably impudent. The hood fell back a little, or perhaps she let it fall. She had fair hair and a round face, pink-cheeked, that seemed made for merriment.

So much so, that he was bound to smile, and the girl smiled back. She had a dimple at one corner of her mouth. He judged she was about fourteen years old . . .

Thus at Easter, in the year 1534, Harry Medley made the second great decision of these particular months of his life: he would be an ironmaster – and he would have Sir John Furnival's daughter for his wife.

2

Sir John and his Daughter

As courtesy demanded, the strangers were asked home for dinner, and as courtesy demanded, the invitation was not refused. But it was more than good manners that caused the guests to tarry, the hosts to urge that they remain till morning. They were pleased with one another's company.

Dinner that Easter Day was at Mantlemass. Dame Cecily commanded the table; though since she was dowager she should have relinquished her place to her son Simon, the true master of Mantlemass. It was said, however, openly and fondly, that none should be master of that house while Dame Cecily lived, save only Dame Cecily. So she sat with Sir John Furnival on her right hand, her son-in-law Medley on her left. Anne Furnival was placed with the young daughters of the house. Those three sat meekly, but Richard, across the table, knew well that Susannah merely aped her older sisters – within her already, at five years old, there burned a fine spirit of rebellion. He grinned at her, but she only pursed her lips and scowled. So Richard scowled back, then looked towards his brother Piers, whose duty it was today to serve the high table. From his situation, wine jug in hand, behind their uncle Simon's wife, Piers winked rudely – Mistress Mary, poor soul, was nobody's favourite save her husband's. Richard's heart swelled in admiration of Piers, so upright and composed. Whatever happened in their two lives, Richard knew he would never have any quarrel with Piers. And that comforting thought sent his glance to seek Harry, and seek him rather uneasily.

Harry was seated next to his aunt Mary, but he was paying very little attention to her. His ears were all for Sir John; his eyes only for Sir John's young daughter.

'Beyond Severn, you say?' Dame Cecily was exclaiming. 'What a journey! What a journey indeed! And did you see Gloucester, Sir John, and worship in the great church?'

'Worship is growing more and more a private matter,' her guest replied. 'These are strange times, madam, and may grow stranger. No guest house where we rested overnight, be it abbey or priory or convent, but there was fear of change to come.' He looked from Dame Cecily down the length of the table. 'But these are not matters for discussion,' he said.

After that he spoke of more domestic affairs – of his own manor of Easingwell in Kent, of his wife's death a year ago, his fears and concerns for his daughter left motherless. He spoke of his brother, visited at the farthest point of the recent journey, but he did not make clear whether that visit had been the purpose of his travels.

'My brother's lands run to the pale of a forest called Dean. The country is much as this one we know – yet sharper contoured and the trees, to my eye, more various. There is much mineral there – my brother is master, among his many enterprises, of a furnace and forge comparing to our own in the Wealden country. He speaks of other fuels that may be used – as coal. This they scratch from the ground in plenty.'

Richard watched Harry burn red with excitement and knew how hard he found it not to break into the conversation.

'So your young mistress here has seen much of the country,' Dame Cecily said, smiling at Anne – and fatally changing the course of the conversation on one count, while sending it into a most acceptable alternate channel. 'At your age, dear child, I was mewed up like a monkey in a cage!'

'But the monkey did escape!' cried Anne, quite without pertness, yet drawing a breath of disapproval from the young Mallory sisters and their mother, and a suppressed chuckle from their father.

'Aye – she did clim through the bars in time to wed with my father!' Simon Mallory said. 'And lo! here we sit because of it!'

'And how did you think of the world beyond home, child?' Dame Cecily asked Anne Furnival.

'Madam, I did find it very wide,' answered Anne in her clear voice, though shyly now, seeing she had spoken too freely before.

'There was none I cared to leave her with,' Sir John was explaining. 'And she is, I own, a stout young traveller.'

Harry, his eye keen, could see the girl had travelled, for though her colouring was light, she was as rough in the texture of her cheeks and brow as were his country cousins. The spring had come early, it was true, yet they could only have journeyed in harsh weather for much of the time, and riding over roads still broken with the end of winter. It would have been some urgent matter that took Sir John so far at such a season, and not only with his young daughter but with her aged nurse, who must surely have been a drag on them, poor soul.

Later that day, Sir John went with the Medleys to Ghylls Hatch, to see over the horses. His daughter stayed behind at Mantlemass, while Harry was required to attend on the two men and, along with Piers, to show off the horses when asked. Sir John was a graceful rider, and displayed his own paces as well as those of his chosen mounts, when Medley persuaded him to try them. Without any instruction from his father, Piers brought out dainty Proserpine, a bay mare small-made, light-boned, a perfect ride for a man's loved and only daughter.

'If my fortunes were firmer, I should ask to take her home with us,' Sir John said. Only later, when they were indoors, he spoke more freely. 'I am plagued by the oath of supremacy, Master Medley. It is not in my conscience to acknowledge the King as head of the Church in England. But I am hard pressed. I have been a lawyer, and as such a distant servant of Queen Katherine. My loyalty remains to her. Divorce is a solemn and a fearful thing – I cannot accept that any man, king or no, may put away his wife of so many faithful years. It is anathema to me that His Majesty should thus bastardize his daughter, the Lady Mary.' Distressed, he shook his head and laid a hand on Medley's arm. 'I speak treason, and should not do so under any man's roof. Forgive me.'

'You have suffered for your conscience, sir.'

'Not as severely as many. It is said Sir Thomas More shall lose his head if he remain firm – and if he may, then so may any man. My suffering has been mostly in my purse! Indeed, though I rejoiced to kneel in Gloucester – and Salisbury – and Chichester, too – not to mention many a priory church – yet my travelling was another sort of pilgrimage. I went to seek my brother's help.' He paused, then sighed almost comically. 'I hope my petitions to heaven may be better received!'

Harry looked briefly at Piers. He wondered, if the time should come when one was better situated than the other, and help be refused. He thought not. Yet he was wise enough by now to know that men change as they grow, and that maybe in youth Sir John and his brother had believed what he believed now. As if aware of his thought, Piers gave him a brief smile. Harry never returned it, for his attention was caught by what Sir John was saying.

'Truly, he did offer handsomely for the wardship of my daughter, saying he would see her solidly wed and settled – and that to all our advantages. But I am soft in head and heart. I could not sell her.'

'Better starve!' cried Harry, loud and rude; for he had broken out into a sweat that turned him first red then white.

'Well, so we may do yet,' Sir John answered, but coldly and drawing himself together as if against attack. He turned his shoulder on the young man thereafter, addressing himself altogether to his father. And though he could not escape Harry's escort back to Mantlemass, there was in any case no sight to be had of Anne.

Next morning, the visitors were off almost at first light. Harry had seen how that might be and was waiting when they came from the house, waved on by most of the household.

'Now you will do well,' said Dame Cecily, 'for here's my grandson, Harry Medley, to set you on your road!'

Sir John protested that he knew the way over the forest and that his horse knew it, too, and would take him home.

'Go with them, Harry,' his grandmother insisted. 'Every stranger believes himself wiser than rough foresters – which is what we are. But rough foresters know better!'

So in spite of the rather testy disavowals of Sir John, Harry did ride with them as guide. Though he had little chance even to look at Anne Furnival, still less to speak to her, he rode home in the late afternoon with his head in the clouds. For at the last, when he had left them and stood to watch them vanish into Kent, she had turned and lifted her hand in farewell . . .

His father was coming indoors with a bit and bridle over his arm and a pair of spurs in his hand. He paused and waited for Harry to join him. He looked stern, which was not what his eldest son wanted to see at that moment. Master Medley held out the spurs in one hand and the bit in the other and shook them at Harry.

'I did forbid these, years gone, Harry. And you know it. This is a cruel bit – ruin to any mouth. As for the spurs –'

'Can I school a horse with my bare heels, sir?'

'Learn from your brother, boy. You'll take a bannicking from Piers, though he be the younger, if he ever see these in the using.'

'Piers is a set-up, stomachy lad, puffed wi' conceit of himself – and you make him so, father. Any about this place knows that,' cried Harry, instantly forgetting his brotherly thoughts of yesterday and caring little if his accusations were wild so long as they hurt his father. Anger made his eyes smart, anger and disappointment. He had seen himself manfully striding to his father with the news that he had chosen a bride and all must now be concerned with the winning of her. Instead he found himself rebuked not only like some silly child, but like some silly child entirely losing his temper.

'A pox on all horseflesh!' he cried. 'Let all rot, I say. There's better things in the world.'

'Softer, maybe. Demanding less.'

'No, harder! Harder! Hard as – hard as stone.'

Let him make what he likes of that, he said to himself as he stamped off, knowing too well that before things became easy again he would be bound to ask his father's pardon for his brutish behaviour.

Piers took Richard fishing and they spoke of Harry.

'He's set to get wed,' said Piers. He laughed, clapping his hand over his mouth. It struck him as altogether comic that his brother was so suddenly grown to a man, when only two weeks ago they had fought like terriers over who should wear the shabby old red cap that had belonged to their grandfather. Dame Cecily had given it to Harry, but Piers, confident that he was her favourite, laid violent claim to it. Between them, they had almost ripped it to pieces – but Judith had set to and made them each a new one, using a close shorn skin that she had dyed poppy-red. 'Know who he choose, Dickory?' Piers asked his young brother.

'Aye,' said Richard; who knew more about Harry than just that.

'Who tell?' cried Piers, the wind taken out of his sails.

'Tell? I did use my two eyes. Mistress Anne Furnival – who else?'

'None else. And shall she do for our sister, minnow? You'll get no other, surelye, these long years to come. For I'll never get wed till I see my dotage coming on me!'

'There's the old trout,' said Richard, pointing. All this talk of growing and age and change made him uneasy. When the time came, would he ever get himself a wife, shouldered as he was? Maybe he should decide to be a monk, like their uncle, Roger Mallory, who was master of novices at the Priory of St Pancras, a two-hour ride or so away to the south. 'There, look! Look, Piers! There he go!'

'You never answered. Shall Mistress Anne make us a good sister?'

'Good as any. But we come to fish, brother. And all you can say is *Harry* and *Mistress Anne*.'

'I say she has a good smile,' said Piers, unable to let the matter go. 'So let's help Harry, for he'll need it, ask me. Her father's made a poor man and awkward in the way of politics. We're for Harry, then, in what he choose?'

'Aye,' said Richard; but after a hesitation, since he knew that Harry might well have chosen more than just a wife. He thought of the day they had ridden by the iron mill, and saw clear in his mind's eye the half-blinded face of the master founder. Though he recalled that occasion with a shudder, yet the boy lingered over the thought of it. Young as he was, he had seen clearly how a hellish magic lay upon that place.

Busy over their confidences, the brothers stayed a long while by the fishing pool, the sunshine of early May warm on their heads, the shade of small leaves dappling the water, which in a few weeks from now would be deeply shaded for almost half the long day. Along the bank, a kingfisher flashed to its young. Ready to aim at anything moving, Richard picked up a stone – and yelped when Piers seized his wrist and twisted it, so that the stone fell to the ground.

'Never!' said Piers. 'Never in all your days, be they short, be they long. And short they must be, come I catch that arm lifted agin any creature living here wi' us. And that I swear.'

'I never meant –' began Richard, pale at his brother's wrath.

'Did you never hear how our own father's mother would call coneys and squirrels and badgers *cousin?* God's work, she say, must be gently treated.'

Richard thought again of Harry, dark and fierce and flaring into anger at a word. Harry said Piers was soft, and

Richard hotly denied it. But he knew what Harry meant. It did seem soft to deny the pleasure of hitting a moving target, whether flesh, feathers or just another stone tossed up for the sake of being struck before it touched earth again. As for their father's mother – Richard had somehow never thought of him having one, for he was a man on his own, without kin, save what his marriage had brought him . . .

As if their talk of him had somehow drawn him out of doors, Harry came at that moment striding and cheerfully leaping down the long slow bank from Ghylls Hatch. He checked when he saw them, and stood waiting a moment, in case there might be fish rising. Then Piers called out to him, so he came on down and joined them.

'Any sport?'

Piers shook his head, but cheerfully. He was not particularly teased by the fact, since he enjoyed the time for itself more than for its prizes. 'Your two brothers bin speaking of you, Harry. It was *Shall they, shan't they* welcome Mistress Anne Furnival for a sister.'

Harry flushed into the beginning of annoyance. But Piers and Richard both cried out together. 'No mockery!' so his manner eased, and he grinned like any other lout in his tender state of mind.

'Do you give me your hand and word you'll stand by me?'

'I do,' said Piers, holding out his hand. 'And Dickory likewise.' He jerked his head at the boy. 'Give Harry your hand.'

A week or two ago, Harry might have snorted at the little boy's hand so stoutly held out to him. But he was a man drumming up followers, so he took what was offered and was grateful. The three brothers, with great solemnity, made a ceremonial of the business – first shaking hands

each with the other through a three-sided figure, as in a country dance; and then all putting their hands together in a pile, right by left by right, and so on, until all six were clasped together, Richard's a little crushed by the weight and strength of his brothers' grip.

'What's our father say of it?' Piers asked.

'I never spoke yet.'

'Ah – but he know, for all that, I reckon. So – when shall you speak?'

'Soon,' said Harry, backing away slightly from the prospect.

'Come now, Harry Medley! How soon? When?'

'Tonight? After supper?' Harry looked now more hunted than bold.

'Aye, then,' agreed Piers. 'How if Dickory feign sick and swimey? That'll take Judith off to see him cared for and settled in his bed. Then – well, say I get called to some horse needs physicking – I'll have one of the men call me out. Then lo! there'll be naun but Harry Medley left to keep his father company – and all time to speak of what lie nearest to his beating heart ... No mockery!' he said quickly, ducking a move from Harry. 'Remember now,' he told Richard, 'to contrive you look greenish and whey-like at supper – and when I wink at you, then you must clap your stomach and groan. Is it understood?'

'Aye,' said Richard, sending his voice as low as he was able to give weight to his agreement. 'Depend upon your brother Richard, Harry Medley.'

'I know I may,' said Harry, solemn enough. 'And God be praised it's so.'

At supper that night all went as planned. Richard pushed his food from him and held his head, and groaned a bit; Judith was quick to see and quick to draw him from the table – a message came that one of the stablemen needed sore to be advised by Master Piers in a matter of drenches ... So, since the family supped quietly at a small board set up in the parlour off the hall, Harry and his father were soon alone.

'Sir,' said Harry, then, his ordinarily rather rough voice shaking slightly, 'may I speak of a matter –'

'What matter, Harry?'

'A matter near ... A matter near to – near to ...' He could not get it out. 'It is a matter, sir ... Indeed, you're aware of it, could be?' he finished hopefully.

'A matter near to your heart, perhaps?'

'Father –?'

'Do you find me so old and scarcey-witted? Near to your heart. That's the matter. And a matter proper enough, I daresay.'

'I do think so, sir.' It was going more easily than Harry could have hoped and his spirits rose accordingly. 'I come to an age where, sir, I should settle my future. My – my marriage, father. It do loom for me.'

He was pained when his father gave a quick snort of laughter, though his reply was kind.

'Such matters do loom for any man, so I should reckon, Harry. Like death. But, my good son, it all come very neat on the heels of Sir John Furnival's young daughter. And let me bring it forward how few such young creatures have come to your notice. A man need a long gaze, Harry, to see clear the one he most crave after.'

Now it was going badly and Harry's manner sharpened as his anxiety grew, and his speech roughened and stumbled.

'I'm dubersome I'll see any clearer than she, sir. As why should I? What better should I look for? And you approved her father, sir. That come plain to any present when you and Sir John talked together ...'

'Let it go,' said Master Medley, easily enough. 'Let it go.'

'Let *her* go?'

'No great task – since she's not yours to leave. I mean let the notion go.'

The bluster went out of Harry. Though he had thought of nothing but Anne and their future, yet the intensity of his feeling now both amazed and frightened him. What he had expected to be difficult was suddenly becoming impossible. He put his face in his hands, saying very low and quiet. 'By Our Lord's good Lady, by our mother Mary – I cannot.'

Medley was still sitting at the cleared board, with Harry opposite. When his son spoke so quietly, he looked at him with more attention, and what he saw made him sigh. He leant forward to Harry, and spoke of the girl's father, of his troubles, of his state in the world as it stood in that twenty-fifth year of King Henry's reign. Sir John was already a man marked for punishment. He had paid crippling fines for his refusal to speak against Queen Katherine. If he persisted in his determination to refuse the oath admitting and acknowledging the King as head of the Church in England, then he stood in grave danger of being arraigned for treason.

'We live easier here,' Medley said, 'away from the cities and the Court. The demand has not come yet for us to accept or deny the oath – yet I know I shall accept it. I cannot judge if those who resist are saints or fools – but either way they've more courage than I could muster. As I see it, it's best to serve God with none standing between – neither King nor Pope ... But that's treason and heresy both, and best not spoken.'

'How shall it trouble us here – that Sir John Furnival think otherly?'

'When the King speak out,' his father said quietly, 'be it in council, or at table, or, to speak true, in his bed – then it's as if a stone's tossed sharp into the great pool of all England. And at the farthest ring of ripples, Harry, where it come close against the good earthy bank – there stand you and I, and those we live and work with. Once the stone break the water's surface, then none living and none dead shall stop the ripples till they find their mark.'

'Father – she'll leave her home and live here safe with us. What harm could come? I do beg this of you, sir! I do beg it! Else I'll live single till my days' end and never get you any grandson.'

His father was now looking at him with a very strange expression. It was so deep, so loving and so understanding that Harry was checked in his despair.

'What was it I said . . .?'

'I recalled your mother. Just so sharp and set she spoke once – and to her father. Saying she'd wed none other in the world but Medley. Piers is most like her in looks, but you've her high pride and her determination.' He leant back in his chair, then, still remembering, but more easily, less sorrowfully, beginning to smile. 'And as I recall it,' he said, 'her father gave none too soft a reply.'

'Then you can understand, surelye!' cried Harry.

'Oh aye – not a doubt of it! I understand how it was for her father!'

At this point Harry knew he was bound to submit. To his bitter humiliation, he felt as helpless as young Richard, as any stupid child striving against its parent. His mind was full of rebellion. He thought of the iron running a blue seam through the stone of those parts, and how it should make his fortune faster than all the hard work with the horses he somehow could not altogether respect. Was it because they could be broken and ruled that at heart he all but despised them, made meek to carry any burden their masters might lay across their backs? Iron would not be broken, only bent and beaten. Though it might be forced into the shape a man demanded yet it was never quite conquered; what it gave it gave grudgingly, and returned no obedience or devotion to its master. The conflict never ended between man and metal. Harry, too, thought then of his mother, remembered that he had been her *falcon*, but saw himself changing his feathers. Grown from the bird of prey should be the bird of fire, the legendary phoenix. It should rise, not to hover and then to swoop, but rather, fed by spark and flame, to mature in the fire, feeding on the element from which it came ... This fanciful imagining, was perhaps a legacy from those brief days when conceits and fashion in words had been his for the learning in that rich kinsman's London house by the river.

'See you, Harry,' his father was saying, 'let the business rest while we see how the world turns. Later, if Sir John's left to enjoy his peace at Easingwell, and if you've still the same mind – for God knoweth a young man's mind can be a flightsome thing – then we'll get to the matter again. Only one thing I find I'm bound to say: I cannot altogether trust you with a horse – then shall I trust you to deal well with a wife?'

Harry went red and glared at his father. 'She'd be my love. I cannot love horses – not as you and Piers love' em.'

'See you make no boffle, then. And let me know you're set to love at least enough to deal fairly and gently – and so wi' all the world ... Take off that scowl, my son. What should I want but to see you well settled? Be patient. Leave all till spring.'

'Spring! This very spring's not half gone over!'

'It ever do come again,' said Medley. 'That's one thing certain.'

Then Judith returned, and there was no more they could say. In any case, Harry knew the matter was settled.

'I dosed that young master o' yourn for fever, Master Medley,' she said. 'Though I reckon it's naun but a monkey's trick and he's hale enough.'

Judith was about Medley's age. After four years of bitter widowerhood, Judith being there in the house and caring for them all devotedly, he had found consolation with her. She had always loved him, even as a young girl seeing him married to the master's daughter. As Harry watched his father look up at her, he knew how deeply and sincerely that love was now returned. He was filled with bitter jealousy, for it seemed to him then that his father had taken what he was denying to his son.

The spring did indeed come again, and with it hope for more than the regenerating countryside. Harry was with Piers and the saddler, discussing repairs, when Richard came running to say their father was calling for him.

'Go quick, Harry – no doddling! Some news come.'

'What news? How's he looking?' Harry asked cautiously.

'A kind of considering way wi' him,' said Richard; and went red when Piers and Harry and Rob, the saddler, all laughed at his old-mannish manner.

'Father's considering's as good as another man's wisdom,' said Piers. 'Get you in, then, brother Harry. Who knows but Sir John got to writing of marriage settlements.'

Suddenly Harry wondered. Might his father have been in correspondence with Sir John? Had he after all decided to sound out how matters might stand? Harry arrived in his father's presence hardly breathing from the speed of his coming and the dread of disappointment.

There stood Master Medley, by the window looking

towards the stable yard, with a letter in his hand and the sun falling bright on the page.

'Harry?'

'Yes, sir. The little brother say you send for me.'

'Here's a thing might please you. Word from Sir John Furnival. Let live in peace, he tell; and all very quiet at Easingwell. Sir John would learn of any small riding horse we might have to suit his daughter. To be a gift from her godmother, so he say here.' Medley flicked a glance over the top of the letter. 'I trust she be a well and wealthy dame!'

'Proserpine!' said Harry instantly. 'She must have Proserpine. None other.'

Sir John had written that the servant bearing the letter could be trusted to lead an animal back with him. But laying the letter aside, Master Medley said the arrangement was little to his taste. 'What other means could you think of, Harry?'

Now Harry was broadly grinning, for he saw plainly what was in his father's mind. He was taut with excitement, with anticipation of where this was carrying him.

'Should I not go myself to Easingwell?'

'So I thought,' agreed his father. 'I see you are still set in the same course – there's no change of heart since this was last spoke of?'

'None.'

'Well, then – so be it. Tomorrow, early. You shall take Proserpine to Easingwell. But best, I do most earnestly believe, that your wise old father go along with you.'

3

At Easingwell

Next morning, they were off early, having sent Sir John's servant ahead the day before with news of their coming. Harry thought this was dangerous, a warning, if Sir John cared to heed it, that he should send his daughter elsewhere. But his father, who was all for manners, in the best old-fashioned way, said it mattered little if the maid were absent, since their business was with her father – or maybe her godmother, who was making the gift. But he gave his eldest son a sly look as he said it.

Piers and Richard stood to watch them go, Master Medley riding fine, strong Theseus, Harry his usual oversized choice, with young Colin Crutten from the stables leading the elegant Proserpine.

'My father never took me so far riding at his side,' said Richard, as they lost sight of the riders and turned away.

'No, nor me. Fortunate brother, Harry, then. But he's the eldest, and the heir, surelye.' Piers sighed and shook his head. 'I'll say it out loud – I wish he'd more loving care for animals.'

'He's a love of other matters.'

'For sure – Mistress Anne Furnival!'

'No,' said Richard, unable to keep the secret any longer. 'Did he never say to you, brother, how he crave to work the iron?'

'Hinted. I never took much count. And best it be forgotten. We should all work together.' He frowned. 'When did he tell of this?'

'It were long since, and naun ever come of it, so I never should've spoke. Keep mum on me, Piers,' said Richard . . .

The spring day was chilly and sunless, so that the new green seemed to shiver and withdraw. Master Medley rode with his usual grace, and Harry consciously set out to match him – but big Jove, a heavy shouldered black, had more strength than grace. Harry rode him with care and command, anxious to impress his father with the patience and skill – at least the skill – which was there for the using when he thought about it. Today he had sworn to be courteous in all things, not to raise his voice, to keep a serene and smiling face – though not a grinning one – and to deal respectfully with his elders. He rode also with some pride. He had never travelled so far abroad with his father before – his uncle, Simon Mallory, had taken him to London those several years ago – therefore he felt his status as the eldest son increasing with every league from home. The sight of Colin, with Proserpine, respectfully in the rear, added to Harry's general conceit of himself. His life was moving into a new phase and he felt that not only he and his father knew it, but even the young servant.

'We'll ride by Tillow Holt,' Master Medley said, 'and see how Davy fares.'

Tillow Holt was an outlying farmstead attached to Mantlemass. The Mallorys had always grazed a few sheep there, for it was on the very fringes of the forest, where year by year increasing pasture was won.

'Why, m-m-master!' Davy stammered, running out to greet them grinning with pleasure, bowing and bobbing and looking like some gnarled dwarfish spirit. 'How goo the world, th-th-th-then, ma-master?'

'Well enough, Davy. And how with you?'

'The ewes lambed down, and my own c-c-c-cow have c-c-calved very pretty.'

Medley and Harry went to inspect the lambs. One of the ewes looked in doubtful shape after the birth, but Davy was sure she would right herself.

'Her belly swarve up ag-ag-agin, when she drop the lamb – but her'll mend.'

'That I doubt,' Medley answered. 'But see the best be done. Wasted animals is sad bad husbandry.'

The delay was of less than an hour, but Harry felt as if they had dawdled half the day. It was his father's purpose, in any case, to take the journey gently, for the sake of the young Proserpine. They were to overnight at some suitably situated inn that would leave them only a few miles to cover in the morning. Harry saw the sense of this – the little mare must arrive in perfect condition. Yet as the journey drew itself out, he was hard pressed to keep his vow of patience.

In the afternoon the weather improved, a thin sunshine gentled the soft air. Dropping often to a walk, they shifted over the countryside with what could only seem a dreadful leisure. Master Medley did not speak much, but seemed withdrawn into his own thoughts. It was not until they had reached their inn, with the horses stabled and Colin installed in the loft above, that Medley came out of his musing and talked to Harry over their supper.

'I came this way once before. But then I was a lad. Younger than you, Harry. For all that, set on very surely to wed with your mother.' He paused and smiled. 'I dursen't have said as much to you, save that here we are journeying to Easingwell. I made a hard bargain a year ago – I know it. But fathers will mostly curmudgeon over their children's marriages, however it may go in the end.'

'I see you did right, sir,' said Harry, mellow at the end of the day. 'How was it you come this way, then, those years ago?'

'I was seeking my father,' Medley answered. 'Who had left my mother and me long since. And Master Lewis Mallory needed to know something of the reason, if he was ever to give me his only daughter ... I cannot tell you all that tale, Harry. I shall tell it to you one day, you being the eldest son – and you shall tell it to your eldest. But not yet. He never wed my mother – that I bluv you know. But it was all for the care of us. Strange it seem, but there was more honour than dishonour. Master Lewis Mallory, God rest him, could understand, and so I came to marry your mother. But from that day I never did use any name but only what was give me in baptism. We have dwelt in quiet close places, and none has ever seemed to scorn me. Nor need you scorn my father, Harry. I promise you that. Never fear what the worldly, with their arms on their 'scutcheons and their pride in blood, call the *bend sinister.* It can be a kind of honour, see you, to be called left-handed.'

Harry had not known how to answer all this. He lay awake a long time in the grubby little chamber above the inn kitchen, listening to his father's easy breathing, and wondering when he might learn more. He had known they were only one generation deep, a family in its beginnings, but solidly supported by the Mallory connection. On their mother's side there was gentry enough and to spare – he would not forget his escape from the great grand London house back to the things and the place and the people that he knew – easy, rough, tough and devoted. He had run first to his grandmother, fearing his father's wrath. Yet he had not been angry, and Harry had never questioned that in sending him to London, his father had done what he thought to be best. Questioning came later, when he had had a year or two to grow; and it came then hard and stubborn …

By morning, after a dismal night, Harry was white-cheeked and hollow-eyed at the prospect of the day's coming encounter. He shoved away his breakfast ale and groaned.

'Eat bread then, for God's good sake,' his father urged. 'You do look most particular boy, pathery and sheepish. I'll not have you turn swimey in front of Sir John!'

The mockery was all very well in its way, and he took it, saying only, in a hoarse voice. 'Sir – let be.'

They reached the manor of Easingwell after some inquiry and delays, seeing it first from the summit of a low hill. The house itself was on flat ground, a somewhat ancient building, very sturdy, since it belonged to times when a man had need to fortify himself against ill-doers. It stood square, with a gatehouse, a moat and a drawbridge. The sight alarmed Harry, for he felt that Sir John, at a moment's impulse, might up the bridge and down the portcullis and shut out importunate suitors for as long as he pleased.

'Take Proserpine, Harry,' said Medley. 'Colin – do you ride on and tell of our coming.'

Within seconds, it seemed, Easingwell had sprung into life, needing only a few ladies in hats with veils waving from the battlements, to appear as busy as a picture painted down the margin of some fine book. Servants ran hither and yon, Sir John Furnival himself crossed the bridge to escort them in, and soon the horses were clattering in the courtyard.

'This is the mare?' Sir John said, when greetings were done with and a cup of wine handed.

'Proserpine, sir,' said Harry. 'A very sweet temper. A gentle mouth and a gentler action. My brother Piers had the handling of her.'

'Your brother! A somewhat youthful master of horse, I think.'

'But none better – my father shall tell you,' said Harry; half because he was beginning to feel a great gush of goodwill towards all the world, and half, he was bound to own, to help himself on by a display of generous brotherly love.

They were escorted indoors. The place was cold, draughty on that spring day, and there were many signs of stringency. The servants were shabby, Sir John's own gown much faded. The lack of ornaments, of hangings, books, goblets, dishes, was very noticeable. It seemed likely that Sir John, harried as he had been for his loyalty to the divorced Queen Katherine, had been obliged to sell his treasures to meet his fines. For all that, he seemed far calmer and easier in manner than when he came to Ghylls Hatch and Mantlemass.

At dinner the gift for the daughter of the house was discussed more fully, for her godmother, Dame Alison Vigers, was at table. She was a little, fierce lady, exceedingly deaf, so that the conversation had to be conducted almost at the pitch of every pair of lungs present. Harry guessed that great wealth sustained her. Since her conversation soon proved her orthodoxy, her loyalty to the King, no doubt her patronage was of value to Sir John both politically and materially.

Though the gift was discussed and Proserpine praised, there was no sign at all of Anne Furnival, who was to benefit. Harry thought again that Sir John had better not have been warned of their coming; he had mewed her up somewhere safe. For all that, her father was paying a good deal more attention to Harry Medley than he had done at their earlier meeting; and his cordiality to Harry's father was quite as much as could be asked for.

'Shall your daughter see the little nag, Sir John?' Master Medley suggested, when grace had been said and the board cleared.

Sir John pulled at his beard, which for all his nonconformity was cut like the King's, and said at last that the day being so chill, it was best she did not go out of doors.

But Dame Alison, hearing nothing of this talk, since it was conducted in normal tones, made her own decision.

'Now send at once for my goddaughter, Sir John,' she ordered. 'If the mare is as well as we're told, and she adds her own word – then, God bless the sweet girl, she shall have it!'

Harry stood by Proserpine's head in the courtyard and waited for Anne Furnival. The rest were gathered round – his father, her father, Dame Alison, a number of grooms and servants. The atmosphere was pleasant, the weather had improved and within the shelter of the court, a gentle sun now shining, it was warm enough. Harry saw some movement at a far door, and then Anne was there, with her old bundle of a nurse, and a young maidservant in attendance. Her father held out his hand and she went straight to him, ignoring all the rest, and stood meekly to accept his kiss on her brow.

'Well, daughter,' said Sir John, 'here is the gift that your godmother offers you.'

She looked, not at pretty Proserpine, but rather at the young man holding the creature's bridle. She looked at

Harry Medley, and very slightly smiled, then looked at the ground.

'Do you like what you see, child?' demanded Dame Alison in her loud voice. 'If you do – it is yours. If not – then pack it back home and no hard feelings.'

'Thank you, madam,' said Anne, her gaze now resting somewhere about Proserpine's near front pastern.

'Well? Well, then? Answer me straight. Do you like what you see?'

'Thank you, madam,' said Anne again, but loudly. 'I do indeed like what I see.'

Now she looked up and over Proserpine, and then back to Harry. If they had been elsewhere, he knew they would both have burst out into laughter.

'Shall we saddle up for the lady?' Medley suggested. 'Colin – see to it. My son will show her the creature's paces. Let them ride out a little. Dame Alison will like to see how the mare goes and how she handles.'

If Sir John was a shade *nonplush*, as any there might say, by this high-handed dealing, he did not show it. A certain shrewdness had come into his expression, and with it a half-smile that seemed not merely to accept the situation but almost to welcome it.

'Set her up, then, set her up!' Dame Alison was commanding. 'Let you ride up and down beyond the moat, goddaughter, along the meadow and back. I shall go watch from the little window on the turret stair.'

Anne said, 'Yes godmother. Yes, madam,' and made no effort to verify the arrangement with her father. She moved quickly towards the waiting horse and laid her hand on the pale satin of the animal's beautiful neck. One of the grooms gave a final tug at the girths; then Colin led Proserpine across to the block and Anne mounted.

A year had not so much changed Anne as confirmed

her. Harry saw what he had forgotten, that she would not be a beauty, even at her best. But her spirit seemed to strike out of her, making her eyes shine and her mouth curl into just enough of a smile to stir up the dimple he had noticed the first moment he saw her in Staglye church. But there was more than fun in her eyes. He longed to seize her hand and race away with her, to take her home with him then and there and for ever.

They were face to face, she leaning slightly from the saddle to adjust her stirrup, stooping above him.

Under his breath, Harry said, 'Speak one word . . .'

She spoke it, not boldly, not shyly, but looking honestly into his eyes and very slightly, all but tenderly smiling.

'Harry . . .' she said.

In spite of saying that he hoped Anne Furnival had a rich godmother, and in spite of the fact that Dame Alison was most clearly so, Master Medley bowed away any bargain; the mare was to be freely offered to Dame Alison to do with as she wished.

Harry waited with his teeth hard into his lower lip to see if this would be accepted. He knew that his father and Sir John had talked together indoors while Anne rode Proserpine and Harry ran at her stirrup. Everything hung in the balance as the old lady, listening very hard, looked from Sir John to Harry and then to Anne.

'How do you say, Sir John?' she asked. 'Am I to accept so fine a gift for your daughter? Is it well thought of?'

He hesitated just long enough for Harry's teeth to clench and the blood to come, bringing tears of pain.

'Aye,' said Sir John then. 'Aye, madam. If it please you, then for sure it pleases me.' He smiled at last and held out his hand to Medley. 'I thank you, sir. For Dame Alison and for myself. And for my daughter. And in summer,

Master Medley,' he added, 'it shall be seen to that we ride your way. You must see the mare and know your confidence is not misplaced ...'

Half an hour later, they were riding hard for home, Harry a neck ahead of his father, full of wild spirit and intoxicated with visions of the future. Ready to match him, Medley stretched into a hard gallop, leaving Harry's great horse thundering and snorting. At the top of the long hill he reined in and waited. He was laughing as Harry came up with him, and as they went on side by side they were more like two brothers than father and son – two brothers who had contrived between them a most satisfactory piece of management.

'I feel like some evil old merchant, Harry! An old merchant wi' gold in the lining of my hose and in a shower from my hat! I'm easy pleased, surelye – for what did he tell me? There's naun for a dowry, the poor soul say, solemn and a shade mumchance – naun save a chest o'linen and fine hangings that come to me wi' her mother, rest her soul. I wunna part wi' that to pay my debts, he said. But there's naun beside ... And naun but a fatherless father to my son Harry, I bawl out. And so we settled. And liked one another none the less for being frank, both sides. He'll not let her go at once, Harry – as why should he? You'm both fully young and chuckle-headed. But she's yourn, boy! She's yourn!'

It seemed almost too easy. Harry frowned and was full of sudden unease and foreboding, his lover's spirit a prey to terrible imaginings of disaster, even death. They rode on more soberly, but he could see how his father was still enjoying the successful outcome of the visit. The first of his sons on the way to be settled, a married man, a husband, a father. As they came within sight of Ghylls Hatch,

Medley turned back to Harry, saying, 'Judith shall be happy for you. She thought well of your lady.'

His smile now was a warm and comfortable one. He was returning to his home with a mission well accomplished – and Judith would be pleased. But how would Judith feel – how would she really feel, having ordered the household and cared for them all so tenderly these long years? His father being a widower, Harry's wife would become mistress of Ghylls Hatch; Sir John could only see it so, it would be a part of the settlement, since it could be based on little more. When Anne came as a bride to Ghylls Hatch, Judith's authority must end.

4

Harry and Anne

Harry had to wait another two long years before the marriage was past the planning stage. Though there had been a formal betrothal for the past year, Sir John had begun almost immediately to fuss and prevaricate; and no doubt Master Medley was moved by his behaviour into similar courses – though both fathers knew very well that the contract was bound to be a straight and simple one, with little bargaining power on either side. In the meantime, Harry rode frequently to Easingwell, returning joyful or despondent according to the way Anne looked or her father had behaved. Twice Sir John brought his daughter to visit at Mantlemass; but although Ghylls Hatch was to be her own household, he appeared bent on keeping her from that roof. Harry knew well why this should be. His father was less discreet than he had once been in the matter of Judith – it was just as Harry had secretly feared it might be. Sir John was not easy in greeting Judith, whom Medley treated as his wife, but whom he had never married. What Harry most feared was that there might be some confronting of the issue by Sir John, that Medley would lose his temper, that the marriage to Anne would in consequence never take place. That the problem could be resolved was true – but those solutions Harry could think of were by no means so very welcome.

One warm noon, Harry was down at the fishing pool with Richard, and Piers came running in search of them.

'I may as well come out straight wi' it,' he said, delighted with the news he brought. 'Our father's taking a new wife.'

Of course the wife would be Judith, and rightly so. Richard shouted with pleasure, but now Harry found himself bound to face the implications.

'Anne was to be mistress of Ghylls Hatch ... Now Judith'll be Dame Medley and Anne only Mistress Harry. That's not what her father was promised!'

He left his protesting brothers and went at once to Mantlemass – as any one of them was inclined to do at any time – to seek his grandmother's opinion of the matter.

'It should have been long before this,' she said.

'But see you, madam, how this do change matters for Anne Furnival – for my – my wife. It cannot please Sir John.'

'Fie to that!' Dame Cecily cried. 'You know well it pleases him very little to know how things have stood till now.' She looked fondly into his scowling face, though this was perhaps the least loved of her grandchildren. 'Harry, Harry – deal gentler with your poor father!'

'Judith were born to service at Mantlemass,' Harry said, gritting his teeth. 'A servant and a child of servants in this house.'

'Aye, for sure,' his grandmother agreed, looking less fond. 'She was niece to Meg who was my own servant and nurse to all my children. Dear good Meg! God rest her – I miss her still. She come as near a sister before she died as any I ever had.'

She hoped to shame him, Harry knew; and so she did, but his resentment stayed.

'What shall Anne say to it?' he mumbled.

'You know naun of women, Harry Medley. That maid has twice the heart you give her credit for. And so has Judith – and twice the sense. They'll do well together, mark me ... And how's life to go, my sad boy, if there's no rising in the world? We're all servants – servants to God. Even kings are so.'

He sighed, impatient with this moralizing, in which the old were all too ready to indulge themselves. All the same, he had come to her of his own free will and had best accept her finding. His grandmother was a woman of great rectitude, not a doubt of that – yet he felt in his heart she was too positive in character never to have rebelled. He looked at her almost stealthily, as if to surprise some fault in her which would justify his own.

'And now I have you here at my mercy, grandson,' Dame Cecily said, 'I shall tell you I find you often very stomachy and set-up. Nay – not to me. But your father grieves often.'

'Grieves, madam? For me?'

'He grieves, as any man might – as you may one day – that he lacks the trust of his eldest son.'

'We see different,' Harry said, wanting her to understand, but too proud to plead his case gracefully. 'He sees soft – as my brother Piers does, too. I see hard.'

'Aye, aye,' she agreed, nodding her head, but again looking at him kindly enough. 'You do indeed see hard, Harry Medley ... But we've all a shade of iron in us, surelye, that breed and feed in this countryside.'

At the word *iron*, Harry's whole expression and feeling changed – but there was a sharp end to the conversation.

A flurry of voices outside made Dame Cecily rise at once and go to the door.

'That's my son's voice,' she said. She left the room swiftly, calling out, 'Roger?' Then corrected herself – 'Dom Thomas? Is it you, Father?'

From the outside world, where the turmoil of political and religious chop-and-change made tragedy of many lives, more than a ripple, more than an echo, reached to Mantlemass and Ghylls Hatch. This came through Dame Cecily's high-born kinsmen – Jollands, Digbys – but even more through her second son, Roger. He had been for many years Dom Thomas of the Benedictine Priory of St Pancras; he feared the future. The King was moving harshly these days against the religious houses, which made a sudden visit from Dom Thomas seem dramatic and dangerous.

Harry listened to the talking outside, unwilling to intrude. Then his grandmother called to him.

'Harry – your uncle's here. Come and speak with him.'

Harry saw at once that his uncle was fussed and anxious, and he was usually a man of much calm good humour.

'Fetch your father and brothers here for me, Harry. There are things must be spoken of. Go quickly, then.' Dom Thomas smiled suddenly, breaking into a quick characteristic smile. 'Never dally, nephew. I am bound to get back to St Pancras. Otherly, Father Prior shall hear tales of his Master of Novices at a gallop over the forest like any lewd layman!'

In fact, as the Medleys discovered once they were assembled, he had come to advise against a very dear project of Dame Cecily's. For years she had planned to build a chapel at Mantlemass. It was to be large enough for all those to worship who were dependent on both houses. It would be a burial place for Mallorys and Medleys – Dame Cecily's husband, Lewis Mallory, should be brought back from Staglye church to rest in his own manor, and in due time she would lie again beside him. Last summer they had dug out the foundations of this future building.

Dom Thomas had come to advise his mother that this had best all be forgotten. It was no time for the setting up of private places of worship. Dame Cecily herself might stand in a very poor situation, with her son at the Priory where already there had been one commission. The Prior had been obstinate and in time he would most surely be broken. The eventual fate of the Priory, Dom Thomas said, was almost certainly decided.

'Building a church here involves too much at a time like this,' he said. 'The parish priest from Staglye will surely be the one to bless each stage of the work. And he was one of those who evaded the oath when the King was declared head of the Church.'

Though later he became more cheerful, as if he knew he had assured his mother's safety, yet the Medleys rode home very soberly. The warmth had gone out of the day, there was a chilly air striking now across the forest, and it was good to get home and escape from the weather.

But Harry could not come out of his mood.

'May I speak with you, father? I mean – privately?'

'Aye,' said Medley; but sighed a bit as he went into his own parlour, with Harry on his heels.

'Anne was to be mistress of Ghylls Hatch, sir.'

Medley frowned, 'Judith did say you'd speak so. I said No. You had more kindness and more sense, I said.'

'The sense I see is – we promised one thing, and now we've another to offer.'

'Less? Is what we offer less? You know well how Sir

John frowned on the way of this household. Judith has been my dear solace this many year, and you know that, too. But ever and often as I spoke of marriage, she would say only she *could not take your mother's place.* Now, Harry – think strict on this and tell me your answer. If I should please Sir John wi'out I married Judith – would you have me turn her out of doors?'

Harry went red.

'Why should Anne be put down?'

'Why should Judith be put down?' said his father sharply. 'Anne's a girl of sixteen brief years. Shall she have the ordering of such as Judith? You are the one who put this in my mind – it never was spoke of by any other.'

'Better I have my own household!' cried Harry. 'Then none's to be put down!'

To his surprise, even alarm, he saw that he had shocked his father. Medley's head went up as if he had taken a blow on the chin. The sight appalled Harry, but it excited him too. The feeling of power he experienced set his vanity tingling. His father had ruled all their lives with loving kindness but great firmness. He had never been challenged. He seemed to be looking at his eldest son as if for the first time with wholly open eyes; and Harry felt himself changing under the scrutiny, offering a new face in which was stamped the beginnings of his own eventual authority.

'You are the eldest son,' his father said at last. 'Ghylls Hatch will be yours. Your children shall grow here. You, too, shall have an eldest son.'

He made it sound almost a threat, and Harry heard it and understood, but still had not the humility to withdraw from the quarrel. He thrust in deeper, obliged by his own nature.

'There's more than Ghylls Hatch and horses to give a man a living!'

'To give *us* a living? Medleys?'

'Fortunes made in this countryside can be made hard.'

'Do we make ours so easily?'

'Softly – of flesh and blood, though it be horseflesh. Hard, I say. Iron-hard. Think of it, sir – you'd do well. There it lie in the ground for the taking. A man dig and smelt and beat – and that man's master. A horse'll die, iron's for all time.'

'Man's not. Save by his children.'

'Yours or mine,' cried Harry, 'they'll come to it. Mind me, they'll come to it.'

'I'm to mind you, then?' said Medley, anger beginning.

'The time's going over. There's change – change. What's my uncle just tell us this very day?'

Medley did not answer. Seeing his rage and his distress, the better part of Harry would sooner have comforted him. His mood would not allow it. He pressed home his attack, half hating himself, half hating his father for forcing him to it. The clash of a young stubborn will with an older, steadier determination seemed almost to ring in the room.

'I'll be master of iron, not horses,' Harry said, thrusting out his chin.

His father answered, sharp and cold, 'Your home is here. You are a child – you speak like a child who thinks to run from home. You are bound to me. You've naun but what I choose to give. Master, say you? I'm master here. Let you recall that, Harry, for I fear you forgot. I'm master, I'll live as I choose, wed where I please. You and your wife shall live respected in this household, as any eldest son and his family should by right ... But if ever you and I do truly cross swords, Harry, how so they be forged, then there'll be no quarter. Go, then, come you want it. Go, and no blessing ... Only,' he said, his voice quiet again, 'pray that it never come to such a pass.'

At the change of tone, Harry's eyes might well have filled with tears – but they would still have been half of rage. How the old did prate and preach! How they did use their power without scruple – and then turn to calling on love and duty to soften a son's resolve!

'Well – answer!' his father cried.

'There's naun left to say.'

'Get about your own business, then. Go, now. Go away from me now ... Do as I bid, Harry! I'm still your father, though you care less about being my son.'

Harry clenched his teeth hard and left the room.

The difference was made up long before it could harm either of them too deeply. Yet there was a scar from the encounter and it might never heal right over. The fierce conflict was between two generations, a steady way of thought and a growing way. Too little had changed over the years at Ghylls Hatch – Harry had first thought that when he was several years younger, and now he was sure of it. Only the horses had changed with the demands of the times – fewer for jousting and such sport, more for hunting, for draught; still the war horses, but those less cumbersome as armour lightened and gunpowder seemed likely to impose a limit on cold steel. If ever roads got better made, harder made, Harry thought, then there'd be more carts and coaches, two horses would be enough to transport six or seven people, the demand would decline. Such things needed to be thought about. It was sixty or seventy years since Ghylls Hatch was set up by Master Orlebar, whose son had carried on the work. Medleys themselves had been there for over twenty years. Surely a man was not born to stay for ever on the same ground? Harry had no desire to move among the great, but the determination to be his own master increased as the time moved on towards his marriage. That would be in November.

The other marriage had taken place already; Medley and Judith had ridden unattended to the Priory on a morning of sunshine, and Dom Thomas had performed the ceremony. When Sir John Furnival heard of it, he sent a servant from Easingwell with gifts and good wishes, and there was a silk embroidered kerchief from Anne that she had stitched herself, with twined initials in one corner. Harry was left to wonder at his own angry fears that were proved so groundless.

They were to set out from Ghylls Hatch early on the day before Harry's wedding. A train of ten servants had new liveries. There had been some irreverence and laughter from Piers over this, since the tenth man was a thin fellow, substituted for a more solid body when the cloth ran out. Piers and Richard had submitted fairly gracefully to the bother of fitting and trying new doublets and hose for themselves; they were prepared to endure discomfort in order not to disgrace Harry. Master Medley had brought out for the occasion the fine gold chain that had been left to him in the will of his father-in-law, Lewis Mallory. It was heavy-linked and bore a great gold medallion, and he had never before found occasion grand enough to wear it. Judith, too, appearing in company for the first time as his wife, was to look as never in her life before, her gown cut from a length of embroidered cloth that Medley had ridden to London to buy. From Mantlemass, there would be Dame Cecily, Simon Mallory and his wife, Mary; and their eldest daughter, Margaret, now fifteen and quite ready to be shown to another world than her own. The Mantlemass servants, too, had new liveries, with on the breast the Mallory emblem, a bird flying with a spray of leaves in its beak, that was called *the lark and the laurel.* With pack horses bearing gifts, with all tomorrow's finery folded in baskets, the train would be an impressive one . . .

On the eve of their setting out, when all was bustling into readiness for the great occasion, Matthew Ade, the head stableman, came seeking Piers.

'There's Sola took sick, Master Piers. Best you come see for yourself.'

'Sola!' Piers cried. 'Nay, Matt – not Sola! Do she seem so bad? What come to her?'

'She look more than middling particular. She were ever a delicate, picksome sort, as well you know.'

Sola was Piers's most cherished possession – a fine-boned creature he had reared himself when the mare died in giving birth. That was not so long after his own mother had died when Richard was born, so maybe he put even more into the business than he might ordinarily have done. He was very young at the time, needing help that was readily given, and the foal had survived to be his darling.

'I'll come now,' he said. And turning away from the final preparations, the wrapping and stowing of gifts, the last-minute stitches that Judith was putting into their father's cloak, he ran out to the stables. Sola was spread on the ground. He was almost sure he was going to lose her. 'She'm never dying, Matt?'

'She've a great growth in her belly,' Matthew Ade said. 'I did wonder of it, some months back. She did so droop from a day's jacketing. You saw that.'

'Aye – but then she bettered. That done-over look went quite off.' He crouched beside the mare and took her head against his knee. 'Sola, Sola . . . She look mighty hover, Matt,' he said, as the creature shivered and gave a heaving cough, the spasm contracting her stomach and making her draw up her forelegs.

'Best I slit her throat,' Matthew said, very steadily.

'If any do that, I do it. But give her time, man. Maybe her eye look not too bad.'

Piers stayed on in the stable, and Richard sought him there. He looked in awkwardly and knew, before Piers spoke, what he would have to say.

'You must dance at the wedding wi'out your brother Piers, minnow. Tell Harry for me.'

The joy went out of the coming gaieties for Richard. He did not argue with Piers, seeing it would be useless. He went back to the house and told Harry.

'Father!' shouted Harry in outrage. 'Is my brother Piers to be let stay behind when all the rest ride to my wedding?'

'What now?' said Medley, turning from Judith's ministrations.

'It's his horse!' cried Harry. 'His *horse*! Go to him, sir! He's my groomsman! Shall I be left unattended? A fine fool of a groom! Pray, father – see he come to his senses!'

'Lord, lord!' muttered Master Medley, leaving his cloak in Judith's hands, tossing it back so that she ran the needle into her thumb and shrieked out. '*Lord*!' he said again, but louder.

Medley went to the stable and looked at Sola, but like Piers wanting the best, thought that she might recover. He laid his hand on her, feeling for the swelling Matt had found; but either by the way she was lying, or because he was less skilled, he could find nothing.

'Maybe she mend,' he told Piers, partly because he could not stand the misery in his son's face. 'We'll see by morning. Come you indoors now.'

Piers said nothing, only shook his head. He stayed all night in the stable, and in the morning Sola was still living and had been on her feet once, but then fallen again.

'I'll not leave her, Harry,' said Piers, when the groom came seeking him.

Harry went away at once, not trusting himself to speak. After that, they sent Richard to try once more.

'I'll ride after, could be,' Piers told him, for he looked so cast down. 'Soon as I may, but I can't say when.'

An hour later, they rode off without him.

Once away from Ghylls Hatch and past Mantlemass, Harry put Piers from his mind. He had too much else to think of. The morning was raw, fog over the tops of the trees, then drifting down, lying in the bottoms. So that they rode sometimes below it, sometimes above – when it was as though they picked their way among clouds. What a foolish time for a marriage, Harry thought, who would sooner have made it midsummer, unless it could have been a whole year earlier. But the seasons being strict that kept the land to its rhythm, celebrations had to take their turn. With haysel and harvest, the fruit and the berries and the rootcrops, and then the hops and then the brewing of them, it might be said he was lucky they had not slid on into Advent. After that, the winter would have meant waiting till it ended, and then there would have been Lent – and it would have been only at Easter or after that he could have claimed his bride.

So far, the season had been dryish and the forest tracks were firm, though slippery with the foggy moisture dripping from the trees. Then the fog lifted and the sun came through, thin yet golden, still with some warmth in it to help the riders straighten up and throw back their shoulders. Later still, there was a great brilliance over the countryside, striking off the fallen beech leaves, turning the faded bracken as red as red deer. From riding silently they began to call out to one another. Then one of the servants from Mantlemass, who rode with a lute slung across his

back, began to sing. The first notes were quiet and diffident, but soon he found a fuller voice as the smiles of the cavalcade encouraged him. Then Dame Cecily joined in, her voice still clear and pleasant; and though Mistress Mary did look a shade disapproving, she did not actually check her daughter Margaret's singing out, loud and bright as an angel. Richard, who had always despised her, paid her the honour of moving up to ride alongside, joining his treble with the rest. Their breath rose cloudily on the late autumn air, as if the music took shape.

This time tomorrow, God willing, Harry would be a married man. He had hovered patiently, he had marked his prize, now he would swoop and carry it away. One part of life was over – the falcon's life, of which his mother had lovingly teased him. Whether soon or whether late, he knew that when next he soared it would be not as falcon but phoenix, born out of some ending, out of fire, out of ashes, out of a dead past. As he rode on his way, Harry was twice in love – with Anne Furnival, whom he knew so little, and with his own rash purpose which he knew even less . . .

Now his father rode up beside him and pointed ahead. Far off still, it was possible to see from the height on which they paused, that part of the country where Easingwell stood within its moat. At the expression on his father's face, compounded of affection and encouragement, and yet with a hint of something more about the mouth, a very faintly sly, amused quirk, all Harry's confidence left him. His manhood was in the proving, and at that moment he wished he might escape back to boyish things. Or he wished he were some swaggering gallant with a row of conquered women to assure him confidence in his powers. He gave his father a hunted look which must have told all, for Medley laughed out loud and clapped him on the back.

'Never look so solly, boy! Leave all that for the bride!'

All that he knew of Anne – her appearance, her voice, her nature – fled from Harry's memory. He could not summon her to his imagination. He could not recall at all who it was he must marry, bring home, cherish, watch with his children ... He could not return his father's jollity, but only mumbled, 'Let be,' and kicked up his horse to ride ahead of all the rest. Falcon? Phoenix? Mouse, more like ...

That night, north-east some miles from Easingwell, they were guests of Mistress Mary's brother. He and his wife, his two elder sons and their wives, his unmarried daughter, his youngest son, would all come to swell the number of guests at the wedding. The youngest son must needs be groomsman if Piers had not reached Easingwell by morning.

Light was not far up the sky when the augmented train set out next day. Of this last part of the journey Harry seemed to hear and see nothing, riding alone, so solemn that Dame Cecily checked those who tried to rally him, and for her sake they shrugged and left him in peace. Only Richard at last moved up and rode as close as he dared, trying to be two brothers, but without speaking, without even looking. If Harry understood what the boy was up to, he gave no sign. His mood was like a shroud on him. By the time they came to Easingwell and were in the chapel, he was experiencing something near despair.

The chapel, like the house itself, showed signs of impoverishment. There was, however, a flurry of the bride's kinsmen who had a more prospering air. They surged about the groom so that he seemed to lose sight of his own family. He looked frantically around, still hoping to see Piers, then accepting that it was indeed too late. Then he saw Anne approaching with her father. He saw her, yet he could not quite look at her, taking her hand as required but absently . . .

At that moment everything changed for him. She might have stood trembling with her eyes downcast, as young brides do, but instead she lifted her head and gave him a straight, honest, curiously encouraging look. Her fingers moved against his, firm and reassuring. All that he had forgotten was there before him. As he led her forward, his lack of trust filled him with shame. He led her, not only towards the altar, but towards the future. His shroud fell away and once more he wore his wedding garments.

All that day, the festivities continuing, leading from one moment to the next, bride and groom had no single chance of a word alone. They were for ever dragged apart, performers in an intricate and formal dance, merely touching hands before shifting into the next movement. And when this imagined dance turned to reality, with the boards cleared, the music starting up, still they were separated. The ruthless press of the other dancers ever sped them on down alleyways of swaying or jigging figures, under archways of raised arms, joined hands, up the floor and across it, laughing and calling, shouting as the dances grew wilder and more rustic, the wine more heady. As each dance ended, a fresh partner merrily swept Anne away. All the men must dance with the bride, all the women with the groom, all the company must toast each of them, again and again. Soon flushed faces, wilder movements, raised voices in a hint of quarrelling, told how the time was going over, promising an end to the merriment, a farewell to the guests, a time when husband and wife might at last find themselves alone.

The time came when those guests who would be able to make their way home through a misty moonlight were ready to take their farewells. But they must see the bride and groom safely into bed before they left. If Harry had been drunk as the others, he might not have minded the men helping him out of his wedding suit and into his bedgown, to the accompaniment of banter a good deal more salacious than witty. But he was altogether sober and found it difficult not to punch the heads of his tormentors, so bringing the merriment to ruin – which was all it deserved; though who was he to set himself against common custom for such an occasion as this? He was fleetingly glad that Richard had long ago slid into a corner of the great hall, curled himself against the wall and gone to sleep. Harry might be called soft and pathery in his wits – or however they should describe it in this corner of the country – but he did not want the boy here among the sniggering and the bawling laughter.

Then he was being shoved and jostled along the gallery to the bridal chamber, where Anne would have suffered, he trusted, less at the hands of her attendants than he had done. The women and the girls were all clustered at the door, calling him to bed, reproaching his slowness, giggling in a high-pitched, near hysterical fashion. Over their shoulders through the open door, Harry had a glimpse of Anne, the colour of her nightgown, sitting bolt upright in the huge high bed . . .

The sight of her gave him strength. He shoved off those crowding around him, and hurling himself through the open door he swung it against the lot of them, knocking down some, so that they fell on top of one another, the girls screaming, the men shouting and cursing. Then, they began beating and hammering with their fists on the closed door, shouting out taunts and abuse, so that waiting only to shoot home the bolts, Harry strode to Anne and put his hands over her ears, crying, 'Don't hear them!

Don't listen! Let 'em all go! They've drunk too mucn, the sots!'

They were in fact friends, kinsmen, solid souls to be relied on in everyday affairs; and so they would appear at the next meeting. But at this moment they seemed a horde of tormentors.

Anne pressed Harry's hands over her ears and wept. He found himself crouching beside her on the bed, soothing and holding her, talking to her rather as if she were his child, not his wife. And her utter fatigue, with the warmth of the bed which had been well smoothed with pans, and the gentleness of his manner, his quiet voice, so acted upon her that, with her head pressed against his shoulder, she drooped, then drowsed, then suddenly dropped asleep. With only tenderness in his heart, Harry settled her on the pillows, drew the bed curtains close, and lying down gingerly beside her, pulled up the covers. He dozed in spite of himself, first scowling a little, then grinning at the pass in which he found himself. And he wondered how many others, like Anne, like him, worn out by the day of frenzied celebration, spent their wedding night without so much as a kiss before sleeping.

Both stirred in the very early hours. A glimmer from the lamp burning beyond the drawn bed curtains showed them vaguely where they were. In the utter quiet, no sound intruding, no owl crying over the moon-whitened countryside, they recognized one another with astonishment and with delight.

5

Family Man

A servant of Sir John Furnival's rode from Easingwell to Ghylls Hatch on an autumn day and asked for his master's daughter, Mistress Harry Medley. He had ridden hard, and Matthew Ade, who happened to be crossing the courtyard when he arrived, was concerned for his air of exhaustion. The man seemed ready to fall out of the saddle, and the horse was in shocking condition.

'You rid like a demon, seems me,' said Matthew. 'Whatever come to you that you nigh kill so good a beast?'

'I've news I must give into the ear only of my master's daughter. None beside.'

'Not news to shock her, I trust,' said Matthew frowning. 'She'm a good six month on the way – and this is a child well looked for.'

'As well I know, that serve her father. So let you send one wi' me to speak to her.'

Matthew called up one of the lads and told him to take the man in search of Master Harry's lady. And he stood looking after the two of them, experiencing what he would have called a *hobble*, an uncertainty, a doubtful and uneasy feeling. For anyone knew that men ride faster with bad news than with good.

Harry was indoors with his father and his brother Piers. They were in the small chamber above the hall where all the business of Ghylls Hatch was conducted. There in a great closet were kept all the details of the business – stud books and pedigrees, records of buying, selling, foaling, right back to the day when the Orlebars first came there, long before Bosworth Field and the new line of Tudor kings mounting to the throne of England. Today, father and sons were discussing the matter of Plashets – it was a Medley property and it was the place where Harry had dreamed of starting his iron foundry. There was a good flow of water there to make ponds, and a very valuable seam of mine – of iron ore – ready for the digging and the smelting. In the years since his marriage, Harry's purpose had strengthened as he saw his father very slightly weakening. Medley was able to speak of the possibility, at least. A few months back, at a commission sent to look into forest matters and the whole vexed business of timber in relation to iron, in relation to building supplies, he had listened to neighbouring founders and learnt from them something of the troubles as well as the rewards of the business. Shortly after, at his own suggestion, father and son had gone to London to consult with lawyers in the matters of license and enclosure. Though nothing had emerged from all this, Harry was certain now that the time would come. He had been patient, he would be patient. But when his father let the matter drop, Harry found himself remembering his wife's kinsmen in that far forest of Dean from which she and her father had been journeying when first he saw her. There, too, iron could be had for the digging, and men from this Wealden country about Ghylls Hatch had already moved in that direction. Whole families had shifted, seeking a better living.

Harry was by now a married man of six years' standing, the father of two children and hopefully of a third. He had gained authority and stature, was solid on his own two feet and self-confident in a controlled manner that had taught him how to challenge his father without quarrelling. He felt himself to be the eldest son in a new way, the heir not so much to material things as to his father's lease of life, his charter for living which must in time bear a newer signature.

At this moment, with the messenger from Easingwell pouring out his tale to Anne, father and sons abandoned the matter of Plashets and went on to accountancy, the table soon spread with bills and receipts and leather moneybags. These were affairs in which Medley constantly referred to Piers. If Harry himself had not been detached from the finer points of the business, he might have been moved to extreme irritation. 'Piers, how was it ...? You will know that, Piers ... What was the profit from the sale of Diana's filly?' And so on. As it was, Harry contented himself with clicking his fingers impatiently as their deliberations were held up while Piers made some detailed point about breeding – the mistake they had made in letting Garnet sire Merope's last foal, instead of putting her as usual to Apollo. The two strains had mingled well enough in the past, but now seemed less suited – but there, Merope had not been of their own breeding and lacked stamina. So now here she was, dam to a creature of which so little could be expected it had best be dispatched and forgotten ... And so it went on, Piers in gloomy mood, as so often nowadays. He had reason, certainly. While Harry's life had run so sweetly since his marriage, Piers's had lost direction. He, too, had taken a wife, and a little daughter was all that was left to him. By his own wish, these things were not spoken of, but they could not be forgotten.

'What I do hate above all else, sir,' he was insisting, still refusing to let the matter go, 'is to make a boffle out o' good horseflesh.'

'The fault was mine,' his father agreed. And very well aware of Harry's growing impatience, he closed the subject. 'Let be, then. The foal goes and I'll be less a fool next time!'

Though Harry no longer allowed himself any resentment at the close relationship between his brother and their father, he disliked this exchange. Nowadays he often thought of that brief stay in London when he was a boy, and he found remembered formalities more to his taste than the easy-going ways of his home. Because of it, and because of a certain self-importance that had come to him since the birth of his son, he was increasingly inclined to drop the easy forest way of speech, and liked his family best when they spoke straighter. Piers, however, grew increasingly rustic, and Master Medley seemed happy to match him. Even at Mantlemass, with Dame Cecily to watch their manners, Piers spoke like a forester and made no apology – though the rest became more courtly the moment they stepped under Dame Cecily's roof.

'That's Merope done with, then,' said Harry. 'So let's get to that Kent sale that brought in less than it should. That was set on by you, brother Piers, as I recall it.'

Before Piers could answer, Anne came running into the room, calling out, 'Harry! Harry! Oh, *Harry*!' and then breaking into loud tears.

'She's ill!' cried Harry, leaping to his feet and all but sweeping the table clear with his sleeve. 'There, my good soul,' he said, enfolding her. 'Tell me! Is it the child?'

'My father, husband! My father! Oh, my poor, poor father!'

'Be calm,' he urged.

'Tell us what you know – quiet, now,' said Master Medley. And he called out, as he always did now in any such moment, 'Where's Judith? Judith shall know what's amiss . . . Stop weeping, daughter. You'll harm yourself.'

Then Judith came in, her skirts swishing, a rock so sure and steady each one of them there instantly dashed himself against it, crying out, 'What's befallen her?' 'She yammers so none can hear what she say!' 'Hush, my dear love, hush! We cannot cure a hurt unseen.'

'Tell them!' Anne cried to Judith. 'I cannot speak of it!'

'There's a servant rid here from Easingwell,' Judith said. 'Lord save all! A man like Sir John! So upright as he is, and honest and gentle . . . I can hardly speak it any more than his daughter may.'

'Aye, for God's sake,' Medley cried, 'one or t'other must find words.'

'He's lying in Maidstone Gaol, sir! Believe it if you are able.'

'On what charge? The old business – after so long?'

'It is!' Anne wailed. 'In part, it is. You know well how it was with him – all but ruined by the great fines set on him – and any others who spoke out for the Lady Mary as he did.'

'Things are better now,' Harry said. 'Long past, the King acknowledged her. She is his true lawful daughter and he has said so. Anyone knows that – if we know it even here! And Sir John has been let live in peace since before you and I got wed.'

'The servant tell of some new inquiry,' Judith said. 'That mean sniffing and snarling after monies – and it do appear Sir John might be said still in debt for his past faults – so they're named.' She put her arms round Anne, who had pulled away from Harry, and held her firmly, soothing and stroking. 'Now cease that bawling, my young mistress. Consider the babe and make an end of your yammering.'

'It's never for old debts her father's flung in prison, surelye,' Piers said. 'So – what other?'

'That "other" do spell out the madness in all men,' Judith cried. 'Be they high, be they low, king or bishop or mere hind. The charge is – he did dare read the Bible aloud to his own servants in his own hall! He did wi' all the love and respect that's in him read the Bible in English! And this, I now learn, is become a crime.'

'How should it be so?' Master Medley frowned. 'We hardly had it give us in English – and now shall it be taken away? I find no understanding of this.'

'Father Oswald did speak something of the sort, sir,' Harry reminded him. 'You remember, Piers?'

'Something . . .'

'It was now named a grave fault, he said, to read such in church, or to any less than a gentleman's own family in that gentleman's own home – but no servants should hear it, nor any woman save the mistress of the house, because of heresies there could be in the new language – in changing the language, see you.'

'He will die!' cried Anne, in a great new burst of weeping. 'My father's nor young nor strong. If he be not condemned, yet he'll take fever in gaol. I am as good as orphaned!'

'And your children shall be motherless, come you screech so!' Judith promised her. 'Come to the kitchen. I shall brew you a good posset. Come now, let these brave men see what's to be done. Come with me, Anne.'

'Sir!' cried Anne, breaking from Judith and running to Medley, slipping warm loving arms round his neck. 'Sir – my other father . . . Pray help him!'

'I shall, I shall!' he said, returning her embrace and

kissing her fondly. 'Now go with Judith and be careful of yourself – else must my grandchildren suffer.'

But when the two women had gone, he shook his head.

'Here's the stone in the water, Harry. Didn' I say long since – the King's word drop like a stone in water and there's none living can hold back the ripples it set up. None may quiet the water till the last of the business be done . . . And that's maybe never.'

'I'll go to Easingwell,' Harry said. He sounded firm, but the idea of leaving Anne just now was painful to him. He felt a coward and was certain his reluctance could be heard.

'I shall do that,' his father answered. 'First to Maidstone, rather. After, if need be, to London. I'll go now to speak with your grandmother. We all know she's powerful kin. The Jollands ever did walk warily. Loyal to the Pope or no, they do contrive their consciences and their safety. There's none among 'em, that I recall, ever lost a groat in fines!' He laughed a little at the thought of the careful Jollands. 'Well – come they speak up if need be, God save their consciences, I say!'

Piers would see about horses for the journey. When? Tomorrow? 'Who shall go wi' you? Shall it be Young Will? Or Colin Turner?'

'Maybe Colin . . . we'll speak of it later.'

'I'll come with you to Mantlemass,' Harry said.

His father's firmness touched him. The authority he had so often struggled against suited them both now. It was a long time since Harry had considered his father's origins, therefore his own. He wondered now, in the midst of his anxiety for Sir John, what blood ran in his father's veins other than the good foresty blood that made him so fine a countryman. He seemed at such moments as this to order more by instinct than by the weight and experience of his years. Harry recalled that first time they had ridden together to Easingwell, and how there had been hints of a mystery which might one day be told to the eldest son ... And to his son after ... He looked at his father with affection and with sadness, wondering that it should ever seem needful to challenge him, knowing that it would be needful often and often again before the whole tale was told.

Halfway between Ghylls Hatch and Mantlemass, Harry and his father met Richard on foot. Save for holiday times he had been making that journey twice a day for the past five or six years. He might be kept at home by snow, or he might be kept at Mantlemass by snow, but nothing else kept him. He was fifteen now and suddenly sick of the lessons so diligently given by Austin Woodward, who was the manor clerk and Dame Cecily's valued adviser. But the lessons were shared with his cousin, Susannah Mallory, and that was the reward of their tedium. She was clever and knew it. She had become, not merely highspirited – as when, a small child, she had cast away the meekness her mother preached – but strong and full of good sense, of wit. Richard loved her dearly – but whether as cousin, as sister in learning, as lively companion, or in some other fashion, he would consider later on ...

Richard ran to meet the horses, then turned back the way he had come and jogged at his father's stirrup, so that when Master Medley suddenly reined in, Richard all but fell flat on his back.

'Get back home, Richard. Tell Piers I've chose my travelling companion. Let it be young Colin in attendance. Say you are to come with me and may choose what mount you please.'

Richard could not imagine what his father was talking

about, still less that he meant what he said. He saw Harry frown and open his mouth in protest, then close it hard.

'Sir . . .? Tell Piers . . . What mount, father? Colin to go wi' you on some journey? And – and I . . .? Well, what journey, sir?'

'A heggling, mortacious, dismal journey, could be. I'll need a spry companion to keep my soul easy. Get you home, then, and tell Piers what I say.'

He kicked up his horse and sprang away, leaving his youngest son gaping, half in delight and half in alarm, staring after the two horsemen until the rise of the ground and the turn of the track received them from view. Then he ran for home, hunching his shoulders as always when he was excited.

'Now he got three grown sons,' was what Piers said, when Richard took him the news. He smiled at the youngest brother, then seized him by the hair and wildly roughed it till it stood on end. But when Richard bellowed, Piers hushed him. 'Keep mum, a little. Anne's sore frit wi' news of her father. You get indoors and tell Judith what's set for tomorrer.'

He shoved the boy on his way, glad for his pleasure in the coming journey, but sorrowful, too. He understood his father's decision, for it was time that Richard grew up. Because of his shoulder, which did check him a little in chosen pursuits, they had all but Harry inclined to spoil him, and that had kept him young. There was a new generation now. Richard must move on and let the newcomers into the place he had kept warm for them, perhaps too long. Yet because Piers himself had experienced great shock and sorrow, he wished that Richard's first trip from home might have been a happier occasion. He feared what might appear of Sir John Furnival's situation; he did not care to think of Richard faced all at once with the disaster, perhaps even the brutal destruction, of a man he knew and had openly admired.

It was a very quiet day, the autumn still in full fire, though the feast of All Saints was more than a week past. Such days, here about the forest, days when the season seemed to consume itself, were days of strange suspense, of uncertain tomorrows. As if, in this stillness, there lay a choice directly granted from heaven. Yet that choice was bound always to be a wrong one, and because of it melancholy and disappointment already tinged both light and shadow.

Piers turned impatiently from all this, and from thoughts of Harry, of their father, of Sir John in his prison cell. He went indoors. Before the fire he would find Anne and Judith, the children with their nurses: his own motherless five-year-old, Catherine, and Harry's two – his daughter, Cecily Anne, his son, another Harry, but to avoid confusion called *Jack* by the family, his second name having been given in compliment to his maternal grandfather.

Anne cried out when Piers came in, 'Is there news, brother? Have they come home with news?'

'Give 'em time,' he said. 'They're barely settled safe under my grandmother's roof. And there'll be much to decide, I reckon.'

'Patience,' said Judith, who was sitting with Catherine pulled against her knee. She gave the child a little shove. 'Go greet your father, nice and mannerly,' she said.

Catherine stood hesitating. She had been a fine, smiling baby, but she had grown lately oddly reserved for so young a creature. Perhaps he should not have brought her home, Piers sometimes thought, but left her happy with her foster-mother in Kent. He held out his hand to her. 'Come now – put your hand here where I've put mine.'

Still Catherine held back. It was her cousin, Cecily Anne, most often called Cecilia, older and merrier, her own father's best darling and knowing it very well, who thrust past and threw herself, laughing and beguiling, into Piers's arms.

'What's this?' he cried. 'Ask for a daughter and get sent a niece? A gimsy girl, surelye, but not my Catherine!'

Then Catherine moved slowly towards him, and made him a courtesy, as she had been taught, but without a smile. Over the children's heads he caught Judith's glance and saw that she was troubled. And he was troubled, too, thinking of his daughter's young mother, so early lost . . .

It was dusk when Harry returned.

'My father stays at Mantlemass overnight. There are letters need to be written – so Dame Cecily is about it. She's set on to address her kinsmen in London.'

'If he must go pleading to London,' said Anne, 'my poor father shall lie long at Maidstone.'

'Well, it will be Maidstone first – that's clear. That shall put some heart into Sir John. But there's none there to bargain with.' He urged her, as the others had done, to be patient.

A gloom settled over them, gathered there by the fire. The childen were taken away to their beds. Anne sat weeping quietly and Harry could not comfort her. She was usually so smiling a girl that the change in her was doubly pitiful.

Next morning, both Harry and Piers went with Richard to Mantlemass, to see him and their father on the way. The morning was bright, the sorrow had faded from the trees and the far banks. The prospect of some action made them all more cheerful and it became less necessary for Richard to conceal his pleasure at setting out as his father's travelling companion.

It was harder for those left behind.

'We'll have a starky time keeping my wife cheerful,' Harry said. 'Lord knoweth how long our father's likely to be on the road. If he move on to London – and he surely will – a fierce winter could keep him there till spring.'

'Well, then, Harry,' Piers said at once, 'the eldest son do be master. I'll answer to your word, gladly as his.'

Harry nodded, but did not thank him. It was proper that he should be in command in their father's absence, and the circumstances should make it a very sober responsible matter. He wished he need not feel a stir of excitement, and anticipation of power. Would Piers be so reasonable, he wondered, without generosity, only shrewdness, if their father had left them for ever, if the eldest son had indeed rightfully inherited and become master? There would be all the trouble of their divided interests – horseflesh, iron. Before he knew it, Harry was halfway to the thought that without their father to stand with them – and it was indeed *with*, not *between* – he and Piers might need to part company. Returning from Mantlemass, he had contemplated the vastness of the Ghylls Hatch enterprise and seen that what was here belonged by the rights of nature to Piers.

On this day Harry knew in the quietest places of his mind that he thought increasingly of that other forest, where he could be master, not in default of his father, but by his own authority.

6

Harry and Piers

Soon the fire went out of the autumn and the November days turned colourless – a cold grey sky by day, frost and bright stars at night, no rain, so the tracks stayed hard. At Ghylls Hatch the time was given to repairs – walls, roofs, fences. They were busy as countrymen must always be at such times, when they have won some time from a winter holding off, yet know the threat of its swift coming to be ever present. Work was hard and concentrated, the short day too soon over, yet so full as to be always thankfully concluded. Harry Medley was master over these times, and his power, though it might be brief, yet seemed to enlarge him. He walked firmer; it might be said that his shadow lengthened. In a large measure this was due to Piers, who had the gift of faultless and unfaltering loyalty. Harry knew this. He knew he himself would always command a little by fear, while his brother earned from both man and beast an obedience based in devotion. By now Harry was able to accept his own particular methods of dominance; a reverse side was seen only in his dealings with his wife and children, for whom he had no harshness. Anne had his measure, and he knew it, and laughed over it easily enough.

Twelve days after Richad and his father had set out for Maidstone, the boy returned alone. Harry had gone to the town, taking Cecily Anne on his saddle, for he had promised her a plaything for Christmas, and there was a fair that day. So it was Piers who first saw Richard and welcomed him home with relief.

'I feared you'd gone at least to Lunnon; maybe overseas!'

'It's our father's gone riding to the city – and Colin with'm. And I'm to tell my sister Anne that her father does well at present. He said so himself.'

'Come in, then, and speak with her. Here's Rafe can take Breeze. Come you in, Dickory. You rid so far on your own?'

'Aye,' said Richard, satisfaction in his tone, but walking a shade bow-legged. 'Breeze never falter. There's a mare well named, brother – for she carried me easy as the wind since early morning.' He swaggered enough for Piers to laugh out loud. 'I'm hungry for ten,' boasted Richard.

They found Anne with Judith, busy about still-room work, storing away bags of dried herbs that they had been rubbing off their stalks over the last hour or so.

'Here comes Richard,' Judith said, the first to look up. She put her hand on Anne's wrist, saying, 'Speak calmly.'

Anne turned, wiping her hands on her apron. The air was pungent with the scent of the herbs, and chilly as a vault. Anne put away Judith's hand and said very quietly, 'Come to the fire, Dickory.' She led the way into the warm kitchen. The maids were in the midst of a day's baking, their hair wisping out from their caps and kerchiefs, their faces crimson from the heat of the ovens. 'Tell me here,' Anne said. 'Did you see him? How does he look? Has your father gone to London? Did there seem some hope?'

'Sister! How shall I answer first? Yes – my father is gone to London – and, yes, I did see yourn. And he's well enough, he say to tell you – to be sure to tell you. Tell her I'm well enough, he said.'

'What more?'

'There's little. Only he tell you, take care of his grandson that's coming.'

Anne put her hand on her stomach, almost as if in this way she passed the message to the unborn baby. She smiled slightly, but it was a poor effort.

'So he must stay in prison, then.' She turned away, saying in a voice that would easily break into tears, 'The cold winter can only kill him . . .'

'There were many letters writ by Dame Cecily,' Judith reminded her. 'Her kinsmen, some, are close about the Court. Sir John shall be let free long before harm come. Now – go sit warm in the parlour, and set your feet on a stool and rest a little.'

Anne took off her apron and handed it to Judith in an absent way. 'I shall be better soon, Judith. I'll not mope for ever.'

She walked away slowly and they watched her go. Piers said quietly, 'The cold *will* kill him, surelye. I went inside a prison once. Cold is the worst of all. And if a man be not released speedily, then he will be forgot, and stay long – maybe for ever.'

It was the day after this that Piers saw a stranger walking over on the far bank of the forest from Ghylls Hatch. Bare branches gave that winter view which each year at this time seemed new. Piers had gone to look out for Harry, due back about now. The stranger was a small man, both short and narrow. Even at this distance it was possible to see the darkness of his complexion. Dark as a charcoal burner, as a furnace stoker – but darker still than both. Men of such dusky skin came from strange far places, as Piers knew well – and had in fact only ever seen one such till now, and he was in a mountebank's booth at the sheep fair. The stranger paused as Piers watched him. He stood gazing over to Ghylls Hatch, where two of the men were exercising young stock in the big field that ran up towards the stables. After a while, the stranger staring at the horses, Piers staring at the stranger, he moved on and disappeared over the nab, while Piers turned towards the house and was soon indoors.

Dusk was almost down. Harry would not ride in that night. Piers found Anne in a fuss at the little girl being kept away so long.

'They will have stayed with my brother and his wife,' Judith said. 'His wife will play as she may with any child. It's a kindness to stay, for she's none of her own.'

'Let him come soon, then,' said Anne. 'I'll be having the next without he's at home.'

'What should we want wi' him?' cried Judith, gently and easily laughing. 'We'll manage very well on our own. Men have a lowly place to keep at such times.'

Next morning, as soon as the day was well begun, the stranger came again. This time Piers found him in the yard. A knot of men stood watching him, and others had paused in their work and were moving nearer.

Piers, too, stood to watch. The stranger had brought with him a very small black pony, which he led up and down and around, displaying its paces, commanding it so skilfully that it reared and bowed and seemed almost ready to dance for him. Mane and tail were long and flowing, the tail indeed nearly touching the ground. The animal was groomed to perfection, the whole coat gleaming and smooth as a pond at midnight. And it was fantastically trapped, wearing harness with bells, a plume

at the brow, a scarlet saddle cloth with gold embroidery thick along the hem. It seemed a creature out of some magic world.

Beside his gallant little steed, its owner looked a scarecrow. Dirty locks hung forward over his dark face; he wore a cloak in tatters, showing small streaks of faded crimson under the hood thrown back on his shoulders. Yet in his left ear he wore a jewel, as any courtier might, and on his hands, that showed grime though they were already dark, he wore many rings, some plain gold twisted and knotted, and some gleaming with gems. Gold chains hung about his neck, the feather in his hat was pinned with silver and crystal.

'Who is he?' Piers asked Matthew Ade. 'Where's he from?'

'That's a thing I'm not like to answer, master, for I cannot. He come up the track a half-hour gone, and never asked, but brought in the little mare.'

'I never saw its like – or his. Did you, Matt? Both dark as sin. But graceful, both on 'em.'

He was right, for by now man and pony were all but dancing together. Those who were watching began to murmur and then to shout out in admiration, the suspicion vanishing from their faces, and with it, save for a couple of older men, a look almost of fear that the dark face and the capering creature had at first put there.

Piers moved forward, calling out to the man, asking him where he was from.

Instantly, the stranger checked the pony, bowing low to Piers. The animal, too, bowed thrice, the plume on its brow nodding and bounding, while with first one forehoof and then the other, it gracefully pawed the ground.

'I am from over the water, lord,' the man said, his cap snatched off and held in servility against his breast, but also, Piers thought, in mockery.

'An Ottoman?' Piers asked, mouthing the strange word, left in his mind from old tales told of the Crusades, that he had heard in childhood.

The man answered, 'In Outremer a stranger, in Antioch a slave ... The Sultan knoweth my name. Yet I am not born to the Crescent.'

The riddle, smoothly offered, made Piers not so much *nonplush* as suspicious. Now the mockery seemed open and he felt the challenge but did not know how to meet it. He wanted the man away. He wanted him gone before Harry came home, as he might at any moment. He was uncertain why he felt this so strongly, why his unease increased.

'And the mare? Of what breeding?'

'The blood is of Araby, lord, but subtly blended to a smaller strain.'

Piers looked over the pony, but moved no nearer. It was the smallest he had seen, not rough and tough as most small animals at home, but rather a model, a miniature of what was told of Arab horses in travellers' tales. They had often dreamt of using such a strain at Ghylls Hatch, where all but one line was descended from the *great horse* of earlier times, and likely to throw back to that pattern. 'How comes such a creature in your hands?' Piers asked.

'It is for *your* hands, my prince.'

Piers laughed. He found the man's manner increasingly distasteful, and was sure that when the fellow said *my prince*, the youngest lads watching grinned into their sleeves. He stepped back, disassociating himself from any possible dealing.

'A gimsy enough creature, but unfitted for country carrying.' He turned away, saying to Matt Ade, 'See he has food and drink and send him off.'

It was at this moment that Harry Medley, riding his

present favourite, a big blue roan called Memphis, and with his daughter Cecily Anne set up in front, came into the yard by the forest gate. He paused when he saw the crowd. One of the men, instantly aware of Master Harry, ran to take Memphis.

'What's afoot here?' Harry asked, as he dismounted and lifted down the little girl.

'It's some heathen come out the forest, Mus' Harry. And a creature wi' him like a horse wi' wings! A tiny horse, surelye – tiniest ever seen. A merest nidget of a creature, sir!'

Harry took the child by the hand and walked with her across the littered cobbles of the yard, birds pecking at straw and dung, flying up ahead of them, settling down behind. He saw Piers turning sharply away, as if in escape, and shouted out to him – 'Come back! Tell me what's doing.'

'It's naun,' answered Piers, reluctantly returning, and sounding strangely sullen. 'Naun but a toy horse, best forgotten. A plaything. The fellow brought him's all but a blackamoor. I said to Matt to get rid of him.'

'A toy horse, Cecilia!' cried Harry to the child at his side. 'Shall we go look together?'

'Best you're not beguiled, brother,' Piers said, frowning. 'No – nor the little soul, neither.'

'There's more than one Medley can judge a horse, I daresay,' Harry said, shortly, and led the child away, leaving Piers to turn on his heel.

The dark man and his horse stood quietly, with the Ghylls Hatch men melting away back to work before Master Harry should lay his tongue about them. Thus in the yard cleared suddenly of spectators, the Ottoman, as Piers had called him, stood quiet at his horse's head and waited. Then as father and daughter reached him, he bowed lower even than before, sweeping his cap almost to the ground, humbly touching his forehead, and then commanding his creature, too, to obeisance.

The little girl gave a great cry of delight, clasping her hands together and rushing forward; then, seeing the strange dark face, faltering and retreating half into hiding behind her father, peering out as she clutched the hem of his jerkin.

'Why, look – it is a toy indeed!' cried Harry in amazement and admiration. 'How do you come to be here – so far from your own sun?' he demanded of the man, but smiling.

'I am come to seek you, my good lord,' the man answered. 'I am sent. But who sent me cannot be known.'

'Father!' cried Cecilia, dancing up and down, tugging at his jerkin. 'Father – sir – Master Harry Medley, sir' – for she had this way of naming him that made the rest laugh, to her great enjoyment.

'What, my heart?' said Harry; but absently, since he was looking over the quietly standing mare.

But she tugged still, then drew him down to her. She cupped her hands to whisper, and now she had what she had come to expect – his whole attention.

Listening and smiling, holding her against him and doting, Harry said at last. 'Why not? Why not, indeed!' He told the man, 'She asks to be jossed up ... She would try the seat,' he explained, seeing the unfamiliar words could mean nothing. 'Let her do so. She is easy in the saddle, young as she is.'

No saddle could be found that was narrow or light enough, so at last Cecilia was lifted on to the scarlet and gold cloth. The child sat straight, astride like a boy, her skirts to her thighs, and Harry took the rein and began to lead her about the yard. At first Cecilia, her hands wound into the fine mane, looked stern and concentrated. Then she began to smile, to laugh, and with great ease of manner to urge the animal on. Harry laughed back, for the child seemed to him so beautiful he could barely ever look at her without a beaming pride. He began to move faster, from a walk into a jogtrot, until at last he was running, and the horse with its flowing smooth gait was past an amble and somewhere near a canter. Harry began to lose his breath, and halted the ride, but Cecilia clamoured for more. So it was all to do again, until at last he snatched her down and set her on firm ground before she could tease him any further.

'She is an Empress, a child Empress,' the dark man said...

As if by removing himself he might turn the whole matter to unreality, Piers had gone indoors. He tried to concentrate on stable matters, working in the counting house where such business was done. He made a tally of the winter stores, and thought that next year they should put down more ground to oats. Maybe through the winter, if it continued mild, they might contrive to thrust out their boundary, in the surreptitious manner of all foresters. They would be grabbing land from the King, but he could surely spare it. In the middle of it all, Piers paused and covered his face with his hands and prayed for his father's return. He had not known until now that he actually feared Harry as master, however much he might love him as a brother. He was certain that unless his father returned soon some disaster was bound to take place.

Piers had been half an hour or so trying to get some work done, but for ever distracted by his uneasiness, when Anne came in. He saw at once that she was troubled – not distressed, not angry, but disturbed; anxious.

'Piers – have you seen the tiny mare that's in the yard?'

'I said to Harry he should send 'em packing.'

'Well, he has not. But called me out to see. And there was Cecily Anne, riding astride as if she were her own brother, and her legs all showing!'

Piers was glad of a chance to laugh a little at her tone. 'Alack for all modesty, sister! A maid so well grown – quite into her sixth year!'

'I did not like what I saw and have told you so,' said Anne, flushing. 'I am not come here to be mocked.'

'They'll soon be gone.' Piers spoke firmly, to convince himself, too. 'I am sorry for mocking.'

'Pray, brother – go out to Harry. You've a hundred times his sense when there's horses to deal with.'

He rose at once. At the door he put his hand on her shoulder, asking what it was she feared.

'That man. So dark and strange. Like some fiend tempting us.'

'He cannot help his skin – and I can never make mine otherly. One's black, one's white.'

'The animal, then. I fear that. Must it not be enchanted – bewitched? Has a sorcerer not made it?'

Piers felt his flesh creep a fraction at her tone. There were many tales told of such monstrous magicking, and his own apprehension increased because of Anne's words, even though his everyday good sense dismissed it.

'Your fancy cheats you,' he said, anxious to calm her, and smiling as if at some joke. 'I'll go see Harry.'

In the stable yard the scene had changed. Matthew Ade, Sim Awcock, Colin and Peter Crutten, and Peter's son, Giles, were standing together; Harry and the dark man talked a little apart; Cecilia fed hay to the mare that was held by one of the lads. With her bright face against its muzzle, her fair hair almost mingling with the black mane, she lavishly fondled and kissed the pretty, docile little creature.

As Piers crossed the yard, the three parts of the picture were stamped sharp upon his mind's eye. It was as if he drew it in quick detail because he might need to look at it again in the future. Then he saw the dark hand held out, and there were coins counted, the sun shone on gold and the still air rang as metal touched metal.

He called out, as peremptory as his father could sound – 'Harry! Wait! Wait, I say!'

The tone of his brother's voice alone made Harry stiffen.

'Get on your way,' he said to the man, expecting to see him scuttle off with his gains. But he retained his dignity, bowing three times – with respect to Harry, with mockery towards Piers; and deepest of all to the animal he was leaving behind. After that, it was indeed as if he made himself invisible, for when it was spoken of later, there was none could remember which way he went. One moment seen, the next entirely vanished . . .

'Call him back!' Piers was shouting as he strode across the yard.

'I want no more of him. I have all I need.'

'Send a lad after'm – send him back his animal.'

'I've paid out good money, brother. Would you have me go back on a bargain?'

'Do as I say – send it after that mountebank who brought it here.'

'The animal's known better ownership, perhaps.'

'We've no call to take in stolen goods.'

'Well, it's all done now, brother. No need to bellow out about it.'

'I'll go myself,' said Piers.

He seized the rein from the groom, and began to lead the mare away. At once Cecilia broke into wild tears and ran at him, tugging his arm, then running alongside, striking at him.

'Have a care!' shouted Harry.

Piers thrust off the little girl, thrust too hard and saw her sprawl on the mucky hard floor of beaten cobble, shrieking at the top of her voice.

Harry swore. He whipped her up and carried her to the house, shouting for Anne, for Judith, for Bessie or Alice or Nan. It was Nan who came running, for she was most concerned with Cecilia's care – though any one of them might have been named her nurse, since she ruled them all.

'Get her clean,' snapped Harry. 'She's not hurt. Stop your yammering!' he shouted – surprising the child so much that she was instantly silent, and lost all her colour as if he had dealt a mortal blow. 'God's teeth!' swore Harry.

He turned at once and strode after Piers. He could see him halfway down the bank beyond the gates, leading the pony. Harry checked his desire to bellow again, and went after him fast and silent. But the track being steep, he slithered a bit, so that Piers turned. If the horse had not been between them, Harry would have knocked his brother down. As it was, he grabbed at the pony's tail, aware of the ludicrous picture thus presented – a brother at either end. With immense difficulty, Harry controlled his fury and said as quietly as he could manage, 'Piers! Wait – and I'll speak sense to you.'

Piers quieted the pony, which showed signs of prancing, perhaps of kicking.

'Your sense – or mine?'

'What's the bother? I bought the child a toy. You said yourself – *a toy horse.* What's the sin in that, tell if you may.' Harry heard himself losing his gentry speech and the sound increased his anger with Piers at daring to question any action. 'What sort o'fools are we looking – setting up a great belver in sound of our own men? Let be, in God's name. Turn around and come back the way you left.'

'Now hark a bit, Harry – and think steady.'

'I never thought otherly but steady.'

'But here's a grave matter – taking an animal we know naun of – where it come from – how. Who he were who bring it here wi' all that graceful talk. Where might it've bin? If it come by dishonesty from some great house – castle, maybe – how do we stand come it's sought? We stand like robbers, surelye!'

'We're known enough. Who'd bring such a charge agin Ghylls Hatch? Any knows our horses. Any in all the south of England – aye, and beyond that. Any knows who's an honest dealer.'

'Did Matt look her over? Was he careful and sure? Where's she bin, till now? Where's she bin kept? What other beasts jostled and blew on her – what boat was it carried her to these shores?'

'Now what are you dreaming?'

'That horseflesh come quick to disease, same as man. There's striving enough, keeping healthy stock safe and clean at home – wi'out we let in strange blood.'

Harry was now obliged to hang on to his patience or he would have let fly. He pointed out that a man set to sell a horse, sold it for his own advantage in the pink of its form – so why quarrel over so palpably healthy a creature? He said that the pony had trusted its dark faced master, thus proving he was indeed its master. All the bowing and pawing, the tossing of the pretty head, had been performed gracefully and confidently – there was no pulling back, no rolling of the eye.

'Like as not, wi'out that known voice, she'll play her tricks less well. But she'll learn others, and learn 'em for us. So let be how't will – I bought my daughter a riding horse, not a partner to dance with.'

As he spoke, Harry moved to the animal's head, grabbed the rein from Piers and began to pull her round.

'No!' snapped Piers.

'Bring her up back, Piers Medley. The light's chancey here. Bring her up to the yard and look her over for yourself. That is, if you do truly bluv you know more on such matters than even Matt Ade.'

He saw that his brother was stung by that. Piers stood a moment longer staring out over the forest, where the little dark man had vanished as completely as his own shadow. Then he turned back.

'Come I find so much as a blotch on her, Harry – she's dead meat.'

'No mockery,' agreed Harry, very confident.

Piers led the mare into a stall, and she went quietly and gracefully, nuzzling his hand. He called to Rafe to bring a lantern, saying to Matthew Ade that he needs must put his eye on the creature, that none be blamed but he for any later discovered fault.

'Matt saw no fault,' said Harry. 'Eh, Matt?'

'Only she's short a chestnut, left fore-quarter. But I see that once afore and no harm in it.'

Harry watched Piers strip off the animal's elaborate trappings, and then with Rafe holding the lantern close, inspect inch by inch. With clear eyes, good nostrils, firm flesh and straight bone, the pony must surely seem acceptable even to one desiring and expecting perfection. There was just the one scar, where the callous, the *chestnut* or *castor* on her foreleg was curiously missing. Some injury, no doubt, for it looked as if the place had been fired.

'Done, then, Rafe,' Piers said at last. He stood a moment longer, staring over the animal and frowning. Then he turned away.

'Get her a bowl of mash, Rafe,' Harry said. 'No – wait. I'll get my little maid to hand it. Let the creature know her mistress from the start.'

Cecily Anne came in a clean dress, her fears of disappointment swept away, smiling and sweet as a nut. It could hardly be called her own fault that she was grown so confident of her powers.

'Now you shall name her, my own dearie,' said her father. 'What shall she be called?'

'Black,' said Cecilia. 'Black Lady.'

'Call her Lady, then, and keep Black a secret.'

'Yes,' agreed the child, nodding. 'She is Lady, sir.'

That evening after supper, mellow in the knowledge that Piers, the accepted master of horses, had wanted to find a fault in the newcomer and had failed, Harry was bound to press home that he was less a fool than his brother thought him.

'I did see at once the quality that was offered.'

'There'll be no breeding from her. Too small.'

'She is a riding horse for Cecilia. That shall be all her purpose.'

'Harry – I do dread what my father may say.'

'The same as mine!' cried Harry, laughing. 'That the bargain is a good one.'

'If he were home – it never could'a gone this way.'

'But he is not. And it was you said first that the eldest son should be master, and you'd abide by that.'

'Aye,' said Piers; but did not look at him.

His heaviness of manner infuriated Harry. He had done what he wanted and he was certain it was well done. Only it nagged quietly in some quarter of his thought that Piers, when it came to horses, had more knowledge than any of them, having an instinct that was somehow beyond even sight and sound.

7

The Toy Horse

Harry watched his young Cecilia touch Black Lady into a canter, then make a long diagonal across the big field that was called Horndown. She was so young and rode as easily, as confidently, as if she had ten more years to her name. He envied her, for he would never have the skill that was born in this 'beauteous daughter' that Anne had sworn to have for herself before she got to the sterner business of supplying an heir. Her plans, at least, had miscarried: the daughter was her father's child, the boy as yet altogether his mother's. He was standing beside Harry now, kicking at the turf in boredom.

'How say you, Jack,' said his father. 'Shall you be next to have a pony all your own?'

Looking at the ground, the child shook his head.

'Too soon to know what's best for you,' Harry told him. He pulled the boy against him and ruffled up his hair fondly enough. He knew, though, that he had replied too glibly – for here was himself all over again, resisting the easily accepted dictum that a Medley, however young, would be thinking of his horse.

They had made Cecilia a saddle to suit her toy horse,

and she sat now, her mother would say, as a young girl should. Tied with a broad band from the brow, her hair streamed behind her to match Lady's fine flowing tail. As she sped across the field and turned so easily, Harry's delight in her could hardly be contained. Though he held Jack warmly, yet it was his daughter's delight, her glowing cheeks and shining eyes, her childish, clever hands on the rein, that filled him with such pride as he had never known before.

It was in any case a day of great happiness for Harry Medley. It followed triumphantly on a night of pain and anxiety that he would not be likely to forget. At last he had been unable to remain indoors a second longer, but had flung out into the chill of the winter morning and tramped up and down before the house, his arms clutched round him against the cold and against his bitter fears. Then, just as the morning lightened, a window above him was flung open. He looked up and saw Judith leaning from the casement of the room where Anne had been lying so long in labour.

'Come back!' she cried. 'Come indoors, Harry Medley! Your son is born! Your lusty, lovely boy is here and shouting for his father!'

How have women the power to forget their labours, Harry had wondered – for already, when he ran to her bedside, the baby barely clean in her arms, Anne was as radiant as she was white-faced.

'Fetch Cecilia, husband,' she said, though faintly. 'Fetch Jack here to me. Let them see their brother . . .'

Lewis, they would call him; after the grandfather only Harry of the three brothers could clearly remember . . .

So now as he stood watching his daughter and thinking of his two sons, and of the mother of all three, even the weather seemed to increase Harry's contentment.

It was sunny, with a hint of frost, the ground firm but not frozen, the air brisk without sharpness. They were into the new year, still with no snow or any threat of snow. And still no word of Master Medley, no news of Sir John. His father's prolonged absence troubled Harry, but less than it troubled Piers or than Anne fretted over Sir John. For Harry there was the compensation, however shamefaced, of being master in the master's absence, of feeling power as something almost physical gripped in his two hands; of knowing himself, because of it, to be growing in a man's stature – in firmness, in competence.

Cecilia came running back, pulled up too short, went straight between the ears of the startled horse – and with mud all down one cheek, sat up laughing. It was the one thing in which she could have failed him – she might so well have cried at her downfall. He would have comforted her and forgiven her – but he would have been disappointed. In fact it was Jack who cried, while Harry snatched up Cecilia, hugging and kissing her. Then he set her back in the saddle and led her home in triumph, while her brother followed snivelling and snuffling, struggling for attention which never came.

'Now wash your face before you go greet your mother,' Harry urged Cecilia, setting her on her feet again. 'Else what shall be said of your careless father – who let you go rolling in the gubber!'

He watched her gather her skirts into fists and run off fast. He himself led Lady to her stall, then shouted to one of the men to come and see the creature well rubbed down and fed. It was Rafe who appeared, and they stood together considering the mare, who was breathing hard and snorting.

'The little maid set her hard up the bank,' Rafe said. 'Still – she look a bit stalled. I'll see her get a bit more'n her stint.'

Harry then went back towards the house, thinking with pleasure of telling Anne of their daughter's prowess. The place at that hour, the middle of the short winter afternoon, was very quiet, and there was little movement about the forest, where no wind stirred the branches.

Then two horsemen came into view, riding on the track from the north-east. A gentleman and his servant . . .

Master Medley of Ghylls Hatch was home.

As if they had been watching for him ever since the day he left them, first Piers was running, then Richard from nowhere. The men paused at work and went out from the stables and the barn to meet and greet him. By the time they had him near the house, the great door had been hurled open and Judith was rushing as neat as a girl to embrace him, to be embraced. And like any traveller returned, he seemed a little different, not in every respect recognizable – his hair a shade altered in cut, his beard in a different trim, his speech as he greeted them touched by the weeks in London, where voices had another ring. The children – Cecilia, Jack, Catherine – hung back, uncertain if they knew him.

'I never see you in that doublet till this!' cried Judith, feeling the cloth. 'You sprug yourself up, surelye!'

'Come quickly in to Anne, father!' Richard cried. 'There's a new grandson – come here only this very day!'

'That's Harry's tale to tell!' Piers protested. 'Are you well, sir?'

'Well enough . . . There, Harry,' his father said. 'I am home on a good day for you.'

'Aye, sir – good indeed. And good for all us here to see you safe . . . Here's your own grandfather, Cecily Anne. Jack – what have you to say to him?'

Brother and sister stood uncertainly, hand in hand, with

Piers's Catherine even shyer in the background. Then the boldest of the three decided all was well, and threw herself into her grandfather's arms and was lifted to be kissed. That put Jack into a clamour, and even Catherine began to laugh and skip as she waited for her turn.

'Come into the house. Come home, my dear good husband,' Judith said. 'I bin a poor sort o' myself since you left.'

They went indoors, and once into the hall the first excitement was done and the question had to be asked – 'What news of Sir John?'

'Nor the worst nor the best, Harry. I'll tell it first to Anne, as seem fitting.'

By the time they had climbed the stairway, Anne knew already that Master Medley was home. Nan and Bess had run to tell her so, begging her to stay calm, for this was no day for anxieties that might dry her milk.

'Father . . .?' Anne asked at once, calm as she was told to be, but gripping the covers.

'He is out of prison.'

They all cried out in delight and relief. Harry sat beside Anne on the bed and put his arm round her. She began to smile – but she knew, and they all saw she knew, that there must be more to tell.

'Then – where?' she asked.

'Pray for the souls of all Jollands, dead and living,' said Medley. 'It was Dame Cecily's fine kinsmen who saved him.'

Anne broke in – 'Is he home, sir? Is he safe at Easingwell?'

'No, my dearest child. He is in France. There seemed no other safety.'

'Then,' said Anne, 'I'll never see him this side the grave.' Her eyes filled with tears, but she would not let them fall, scrubbing them away angrily. 'But he is alive – he is safe. And so is his grandson and yours, sir. You must be two fathers for me now – I see clear he'll never come safe home to England.' For a second she covered her face with her hands, then she brisked up and said firmly and steadily to Nan, 'Bring my little Lewis here for Master Medley to hold. He is called for Harry's grandfather, sir, for that did seem proper. But, Harry, let him be Lewis Furnival Medley, if you please.'

Harry nodded and kissed her – but he thought they'd have trouble with the parish priest. Furnival, he would say, was no Christian name – there never was a saint called Furnival; nor apostle, nor evangelist, nor prophet, even ... Or would he, the times being so changed, and changing further, keep his scruples to himself? A man's conscience was a tender matter at the best of times, but perhaps never more so than in these strange days.

Harry hoped there need be no difficulties in fulfilling Anne's simple wish. For now that he saw his father once more face to face, he knew there were to be difficulties enough.

They began next morning. The previous evening had been spent listening to the tale of how Hugo Jolland, a cousin at some removes, had set about the matter of Sir John – and how often it had seemed he must fail – how the one best man at Court to be approached fell sick with the petition barely phrased – how it was all to do again with another. 'The King himself signed the release,' Medley said. 'But he did so in anger because one of his ministers counselled against it. It was a royal spite that saved Sir John in the end.' But by the morning home matters had crept in. Cecilia had taken her grandfather by the hand and was cajoling and tugging him towards the stables.

'I have a thing to show, like you never did see before! And that thing is my own, grandfather sir, and shall not never be took away! Quick!' she cried. 'Come quick!' – as he made some play of resisting, pulling her back three paces every time she made two, until she was almost falling over she laughed so much.

Harry followed as far as the yard, then shrugged and let them go. There was nothing he could do to prevent his father seeing Cecilia's toy horse. Besides, he had strenuously resisted the idea that Medley would disapprove, so why should he have changed his mind almost in the first moment of his father's return? He knew it was because his own authority, so pleasant to exercise, was now taken from him and he was left no more powerful than any man's son. Worse, he was reduced to the position of the steward who must now give an account to his master. He stood like a log, looking towards the stables where Medley and Cecilia had vanished hand in hand, waiting for something to happen.

Then his father came out again into the yard. He called his son by name, loudly and harshly. Not Harry.

'Piers!' he shouted.

Piers said, for the tenth time at least, 'The creature did seem made for her.'

'Unknown stock? Come from God knoweth where? To mix and mingle with our own? I never thought to find you act the fool – not where horses was the concern.'

'Sir,' said Harry, also for what seemed the tenth time, 'I did overcome Piers. He was scrupulous. As ever he is – and he well know it. The blame is mine, then. But what harm? Father, what harm in so pleasing the child?'

'More likely harm than good. Mark me, now, Harry – more likely harm than good.'

They were by the entrance to the stable where Lady was stalled, where Piers had gone running when he heard his father's shout. It was strange for Piers to have anything but praise in matters of this kind, and he could hardly have felt more wretched. Harry had indeed overruled him, and though Matt Ade had found the pony sound, and Piers himself had been bound to confirm the opinion, yet there had remained a terrible reserve in his mind. He had known with certainty how his father would respond.

Harry tried again. 'I was master here in your absence, sir. We made a pact, Piers and I, that what I chose, that thing would be. And so it was. Only he fought me over the pony – till I bade him remember what we had agreed.'

'Look her over,' Piers urged. 'I thought her sound. See for yourself if she seem so.'

Medley hesitated. Both brothers knew what he was thinking. He was worried to consider the eager child who had been sent packing while they talked. He recalled her puzzled anxious face as she watched her grandfather's inexplicable anger when she showed him her prize.

'Later,' he said. He went striding back to the house, his rage still all about him, like some great cloak blown back by the wind . . .

'I am sorry, brother,' Harry said.

'Aye. Well – there's naun can be done about it. But if he say the mare must go, there'll be a great bawling and sorrow from your little maid.'

'He'll never find heart to do it,' said Harry, for his own comfort. 'Shall he?'

'He'll do what he see best.'

For the next day or so Master Medley spoke little to his sons save Richard. He did not go near Black Lady's stall. She was exercised somewhat stealthily and Cecilia was told not to speak of her. There was nothing in Medley's relations with the rest of the household to suggest any strain, but Judith and Anne knew very well what was afoot, and neither, knowing the circumstances, was surprised.

When Medley went off to call on Dame Cecily at Mantlemass, to tell her of the help her relations had given in the affair of Anne's father, Judith went with him.

'They'll speak of the matter between them,' she had told Harry. 'Then, if the chance come pat, I'll put in my say.'

Harry thanked her, kissing her cheek, wondering that he should ever have resented her as his father's wife. He watched them ride off, then went in search of Piers. There was a dingy look to the January weather. Harry wished snow would come.

'Work come five times harder,' Piers reminded him, but grinning, since it was work that he loved.

'Not snow, then, maybe – but some frost. Frost enough.'

'Enough?'

'For good health,' said Harry.

Without looking at his brother, he went off about some business or other, he could hardly have said what it should be. He was bitterly uneasy. Of course the tiny mare was sound – hadn't Matt Ade said so, who was wiser even than Piers in the health of horses? Yet there was the one fault – the firing of the chestnut on the left foreleg. It remained as it had been from the start; there was no renewal of the excrescence, as might have been expected. How had the injury, if it were such, come about? Or had there been an infected place for which hot iron was the plain remedy? And if infection – then what infection? Why, in God's name, had they not pressed this question at the outset? He knew well why – they had wanted too much to please the child ... Harry did indeed long for the end of misty, murky weather. Sharp frost was best for the health of wintering animals. Then clean fine air swept through the forest, carrying infections away with it. The north wind was man's friend in matters of health; the south his enemy. Ghylls Hatch stood north and east, but by some freak Mantlemass had been built looking to the south. A madman had done that, anyone would say – though truly none there had ever suffered from the siting or complained of the sun that warmed it in summertime. Still, when Harry came to build his own house, he told himself he would know better than to build it facing southward . . .

When Medley and Judith returned from Mantlemass they brought a train of women with them to see the new baby. Dame Cecily and her daughter-in-law, Mistress Mary Mallory, and the three young Mallory daughters, all bearing gifts. Dame Cecily brought the long robe, finely embroidered, that her own children had worn for their christening. Mistress Mary had three silk bonnets, neatly shaped and stitched; while her daughters each carried a posy of herbs – 'As like as like to the three wise men,' Susannah said, 'save there's no gold!'

So with all these, and with the fond father and the other children, and Judith near by, Anne was all but swamped in loving congratulations.

'And what have you given her, Harry?' Dame Cecily asked. 'What splendid jewel have you given your wife for her pains?'

'Madam,' said Harry, smiling. 'I have given her three: two fine sons and a beautiful daughter!'

'Alas, my poor Anne!' cried Dame Cecily. 'How shall you wear such jewels?'

Anne laughed and said she should surely wear young Lewis on her breast for some time yet.

'Sing the Welcome Carol,' Mistress Mary ordered her

girls, half to change the subject, which she found indelicate, her own infants having been given to nurses.

So they stood in line and sang very sweetly, Elizabeth and Susannah forgetting a few words here and there, and being frowned on by Margaret.

The music, the merriment, the great love and affection that seemed to warm and lighten the room, lightened Harry's spirits, too. When they had all gone and Anne sank back looking weary, he bent over her and promised her she should indeed have fine jewels one day when he was his own master.

'Shall that be spoke of, Harry? Your father shall be master till he die. He is my father, too, and dearly I love him. So I shall not look to that day when there is a new master for Ghylls Hatch.'

Harry was silent. He looked deeply at Anne, and she returned the look honestly.

'I know your thought,' she said at last.

'Then tell me yours.'

'I'll not forget my marriage vows, Harry Medley. Whither thou goest – so they say.'

This time she avoided his eye and he knew she had not answered him.

'Nay, tell me,' he insisted. 'Tell me true.'

'Where should it be? Where should you be master?'

'No further'n Plashets, if my father'd only say Yea. If he will not – then another place. Further. Yes – further.'

She sighed. 'Another day, maybe, that need not seem so far. Childbed's wearying as well as joyous. Dearest Harry – it is all so happy here with Judith and the rest. I'd miss them sore. But it'll be as you decide.'

Just then the baby woke and began to cry. Bess came running to lift him from his swinging cradle and hand him to his mother. Harry went away.

Now his mood had blackened again. He was filled with resentment for the authority he had had to relinquish. He went outside and shouted for Richard, who was somewhere about, he knew. Richard, in fact, was barely out of sight, so he appeared at once, saying, 'No need to go bawling.' Susannah was with him, having hung behind when the rest went home to Mantlemass. Richard was growing taller, and his features hardening into manhood were darkly handsome. Susannah, not beautiful, yet had so lively and bright a face, so sharp an intelligence, that she needed nothing more. They struck Harry suddenly as a very well-looking couple – then Richard made some sudden movement that showed up his thick shoulder, and everything seemed changed. Richard had once said he should never marry and pass on his trouble; and they were first cousins, besides.

'I need a good mouthful of air,' Harry said. 'There's two hours' daylight. Let's ride out. Susannah can have Artemis, if she will.'

'I'd sooner Psyche,' said Susannah, who knew them all as well as she knew her own mind.

'Psyche, then,' said Harry, grinning.

There was no breath of wind on that lowering, faintly misty day. The trees, the dark ground, the curious distance waited. It was winter, yet winter had never truly come and because of it there was a feeling of unease. To miss a season was to leave a hole in time that never could be filled, but because there was nothing to hold back growth and renewal, no ice, no snow, the growing had to begin. Everything that lived, herbage and animal and bird, with distrustful instinct knew that if the enemy came late it must be fought by the young and tender, by the unprepared; yet sap and blood knew no means of holding in check.

Harry was ahead as usual, Richard and Susannah laughing to see him lunge forward on his great strong mount, a big-rumped grey whose nickname was Thunder.

'Where'll he take us?' Susannah asked.

'Where you never went yet – that's my guess.'

'Well, I rid over most places hereabouts,' said Susannah.

At first Richard thought he had been mistaken, for Harry led them by Plashets Piece. There was a cottage tumbled into little more than a heap of stones, and it was there, Richard knew, that their father had been born and lived the first years of his life. Harry was circling the place in a considering fashion, still ahead. Richard knew how he was contemplating the site, measuring with a steady eye, seeing where the river might be dammed, the pond made – there was room, plenty of room, for a moderate-sized iron working, bigger than some, smaller than the best. Now, Richard thought, the arguing will be all to do again. He felt some excitement at the thought – not of coming friction, for after all their father had been much kinder to the idea of iron when last it was mooted by Harry. Richard's stir of interest was more because he could not quite overlook the possibilities himself. He understood what Harry wanted to do, why he wanted to do it. In Richard's case, because he had been frightened early on by the power and cruelty of the iron, there would be less mastering of it than servitude to it, more respect than ambition.

Now Harry was leading them on, and sure enough they came at last above the big ponds of Blackman's mill. The water lay without ripple, holding the sky. The many hovels, the stone house of the founder, had quills of smoke rather than plumes rising into the quiet air. There was no sign of any living thing, not even of the children, and the animals were finding feed enough within the surrounding forest – even the goats and the geese had moved off among the trees. After a long hard spell of work, its rhythm unbroken for days, the fires were down and exhaustion lay even over grass and stone. The whole place slept.

'Do you know what they have done here, Susannah?' Harry said. 'They have cast cannon whole, then bored them through. Same as they did south a bit, just a year ago.' He thought: *I should have been the one.* 'This is a great gift God gave to Englishmen. No enemy must learn of it.'

'How shall they not?' asked Susannah. 'Strangers will come wi' rewards.'

'They'll never buy the guns of forest masters.'

'Maybe they'll buy the masters,' Susannah said, shrewdly. 'Or they'll buy their men.'

Not liking this turn of talk, Harry dismounted, chucked Thunder's rein to Richard, and walked forward to that high ledge from which it was possible to look down on Blackman's. Because the place was still, it seemed to him a picture of itself and of every other such place – not least that one, unknown, unnamed, that he believed he must one day call his own. All the same, he was critical of what he saw, and the founder's house, though it was built solidly of good stone, could not impress him. With the new turn in the technical aspect of iron-founding, men would grow rich, and the masters would not long remain content with dwellings only a shade better than their workmen's. Harry knew he could never be a true handler of iron, for he would come to the craft too late. But others should work for him, and he would master them while they in turn wrought wonders for him out of the element he so admired. In his mind's eye he saw the fine house where he would live with Anne and their children, the servants bustling in and out, the noble horses he would ride while others had the sweat of handling them ... That brought him back to everyday matters – he would not dare speak to his father of such things till the business of the toy horse had been cleared out of the way . . .

At last Richard called to his brother. 'We've had air enough b'now, Harry. Susannah's blowing on her fingers and the dark's not far.'

The stillness and the mystery hanging over the place made Richard uneasy. Maybe Susannah felt the same; for the very instant Harry turned and came back to them, she pulled Psyche round, kicked her up and was away. Richard, unwillingly, stayed till Harry was mounted. Then, as he moved, impatient by now, Harry checked him.

'Wait, Dickory! Answer me something?'

'I know what you shall ask.'

'Well?'

'If you should come to working iron – will I work alongside . . . Is that what you'd say?'

'Near enough. Will you?'

'Aye. And Nay.'

'What's that to tell me? It's a straight choice, no two ways.'

'Aye, if it should be Plashets. Nay, if some distant place.'

'Why need it be so?'

'There's much I'd never leave,' said Richard.

He stirred up Breeze and was off after Susannah before Harry could reply.

8

House Divided

When the weather changed, it changed first to six days of hard, bitter frost. Then it changed again. It began to rain, and the ground, from which the frost had been forced within hours, broke and altered; the surface churned into clods or washed to slime. The rain, once begun, continued almost without let, day after day, until nearly three weeks were past. After the first week, the fall being so great, there were no means of exercising the horses. The paddocks were flooded and even the big fields, Horndown, Scutchetts and Tom's Acre, stood under a foot of water. 'It look like it never sew up proper agin,' Matthew Ade said.

Deprived of her plaything, young Cecilia moped, then rid herself of some disappointment by tormenting her brother Jack, her cousin Catherine. Jack shouted, Catherine cried, Anne scolded. Then Cecilia wept in dark corners of the house, wailing her wretchedness, seeking sympathy of any who might offer it; but all were about their own bothers and she got little kindness.

'Next, she'll fret into a fever,' Nan said to Bess. 'Her father pamper and coddle and all-us must pay for it.'

And sure enough, Cecilia did sicken, with bloodshot eyes and a hot head, a running nose and what Nan called *quilly* skin. Because of the baby, Judith decreed that Anne should keep away. It would have been folly to protest, so Anne kept to the upper part of the house, the old solar and the newer winter parlour that had been made when the Medleys first went to Ghylls Hatch. Jack and Catherine stayed there, too, and they had old Joan Penfold to care for them, with her granddaughter, Alice, and Tom Godsmark, one of the kitchen boys.

Judith rolled Cecilia in warm covers and made her a bed on the settle by the fire in the little chamber off the hall where the women sometimes sewed. All who went in and out stopped to speak to her, to tuck her up warmly when she had tossed off the covers, to throw more wood on the fire. Harry was for ever making excuses to come indoors, and because of it Judith kept him from Anne just as she kept Anne from Cecilia. They might complain of tyranny, but they never defied her, for she was immensely wise in such matters as these. It was she who knew all the simples and remedies, some black and vile, so that the little girl thrust them away.

'Drink, my dawlin',' said Judith. 'Then it shall be the rose honey.'

Cecilia did swallow the gruesome stuff for the sake of what followed, but there was no great improvement to be seen. If she had worked herself up into a sickness at the start, she seemed to know no way to work herself out of it.

'None but thy crossness to blame,' scolded Nan. 'En't it so, Bessie?'

But Bess, less furious than Nan at being separated from the baby, showed a kinder face, crooning over the invalid, sitting beside her to sing songs of country matters, and carols left from Christmas.

The news of Cecilia's continuing sickness reached Mantlemass, and Susannah came through the rain to visit her. Richard was indoors when she came, and it was he who greeted her and took her to see Cecilia. They had all become accustomed to the child at the fireside day after day – 'like any sock-lamb', Piers had told her – so that maybe they saw less the change in her. But Susannah had not been at Ghylls Hatch for some time – perhaps not since the day she and Richard had ridden with Harry to Blackman's.

'What come to you, cousin?' she cried. 'What a poor grizzly mawkin!' She turned to Richard, and she was quite pale with distress. 'They said she'd naun but a rheum! I think she –'

She checked herself, as if realizing she might frighten the child. But it was too late. Cecilia began to cry, and the tears that ran from her eyes were not clear, clean salt tears, but thick and heavy, gummy as a sick cow's long tears.

'Hush!' cried Susannah, much alarmed.

She wiped away the tears on her own kerchief, then looking at what she had done with deep distaste, she threw the cloth on the fire. Then she ran from the room, calling for Judith.

Richard stayed with the frightened child, trying to console and quiet her. And now, for the first time, he too could see that she was far worse than they had supposed. Her eyes were enormous, the irises distended strangely, the eyes themselves seemed almost to be starting from her head. Also her neck was swollen – but then he had seen such a thing in many a child, and a high fever with it, and been glad to avoid it himself. Her skin was blotched, too; though that might be the result of her crying, or it might be the heat from the fire. For a second or two, Richard's teeth chattered, for he wondered if she could have taken the

plague. He remembered that Harry had ridden with her to the town at Christmas time, and that she must have been jostled by a great crowd come from everywhere in search of fairings. It was some weeks since then, but it was known that the plague, though it might strike like a thunderbolt, did also lurk strangely quiet for a long while.

Then Richard recalled something more – that the day on which Harry had taken Cecilia to the fair was the day before the stranger came to Ghylls Hatch with the toy horse they now called Lady. Richard had not seen the man, but Piers had vividly described him – a man from Araby, where the swift fine horses were bred from whose stock Lady had been so expertly culled. He would have travelled through mysterious countries where men spoke with garbled tongues, where they lived as no Englishman knew how, and were prey, no doubt, to many curious, unknown maladies. Richard recalled how the child had mauled and caressed the horse, kissing the soft muzzle, blowing into the fine eager nostrils.

After only a minute or two, forcing himself to crouch by Cecilia and stroke her hot hands that grabbed at him for comfort, Susannah came back with Judith.

Judith had said, 'Fetch your father, Richard,' and he had gone at once. Ever since he was small, Richard thought, he had been sent running to fetch his father to one or other of his elders, for one or another reason – for comfort, for advice, for protection, for hospitality to some unexpected guest, to decide on quarrels, to choose harness. A few years ago he would have gone scuttling, pleased with the errand. Today he went very steadily striding in search of Master Medley, who might be anywhere in the whole of Ghylls Hatch or the near-by forest. Most likely he would be inspecting the horses, feeling their joints, looking at their mouths, quick to spot any trouble. For in such a season, the beasts all stived up under cover, trouble most easily came.

Because of such thoughts, Richard went first to the easternmost stable. But he heard loud voices coming from the disused stable further down the slope – his father's, Harry's – one or other of the men besides Matt Ade – and Piers's softer, lower voice that was none the less emphatic. There was the sound of hooves stamping in a confined space, and a short sharp scream of fear that began and ended all in one, and set distant horses stamping and whinnying. The men shouted among themselves, and as they did so the general noise brought others, to hang about inquisitive, anxious and listening. There was a thud, then, the sound of a horse brought down, but so light there could be no doubt which horse.

As Richard paused, afraid because he thought he knew everything, Harry shoved out of the stall and came almost running past, seemingly without even recognizing his brother. Harry's face was the colour of cheese, and he was so angry it was making him sweat, making his eyes glitter. And he was gone almost as soon as seen.

Then, in turn, Piers emerged. He stood looking back into the stall, and Richard knew what he was seeing, because of how Piers was absently rolling down his sleeve. Besides, there was a spread of blood coming from the stall and tipping towards the kennel that ran down the centre of the open way between the stalls. It looked black, to Richard – in colour and in omen, as black as blood that flows in moonlight.

Piers came towards him slowly, and then paused.

'We done away wi' Cecilia's Lady, Dickory. I felt best I do it myself – I feared another might mommick the job. Poor Harry. I take the blame, too – I did know in my heart. But it's Harry has to tell Cecilia.'

'What come, then?' Richard asked, in terror at so much dread and blood and death. 'He made you do it? Father?'

Piers answered, looking away, 'He think for near-sure that Lady were sick of the farcy.'

Richard almost shouted out, 'Never! No never – never say it, brother! Not here! We never had but once in all the years to say that word! Not our horses, Piers? He never can mean it truly.'

'Ask him, then,' said Piers, sounding altogether weary and out of every hope. 'Where'd Harry go? Which way?'

'To the house. To – to Cecilia, maybe . . .'

'Say your best prayers, Dickory,' Piers muttered. 'We'll need 'em, every word.'

Harry had paused at the door by the time Piers overtook him. He stood like a man trying to ease a burden, to shift its weight before carrying it any further. Piers caught his arm, but Harry shook it off. The brothers stood in silence, while Piers sought Harry's glance and Harry evaded Piers's.

At last Piers said, 'Father seem calm as frore water. We best do samely.'

'Aye,' said Harry. Then he leant against the wall and fetched up a sigh that came, it seemed, as deep as from his very bowels. Then, as if the pressure and the sorrow of that terrible breath might stifle him, he let it go. It came out of him almost as a groan, and he put his two hands to his temples and held his head that might surely burst with the awful burden of guilt that it carried. His teeth were tight clenched and bared, and for a second Piers thought his brother might drop dead from sheer despair.

'Come now, Harry – Harry . . .' said Piers.

'I'm cursed for this,' Harry said, hardly giving the words

sound, then repeating them and repeating them. 'I tell you, Piers, I'm cursed for sure. You did warn me – and I would go my way – I would be master for that time ... Now there's despair for all-us ... Oh dear Lord God strengthen me – let me be forgiven. Let at least my own kin forgive me ...'

'Any cursing,' Piers said firmly, 'it fall on all and all shall endure it and no blame. No blame, Harry. Let that much be certain. Why else did I let you ride me down – and why did our father never see before that the mare were tainted? You know well why. He would not go near for fear – for fear there might be something to make the child unhappy. And so wi' you. And maybe it were weak and fond in each one – yet it were done for love.'

'Think how it may go, Piers. Think!'

'Like it go for others, time and agin.'

'Maybe it's done in time – killing the beast. If not .. There could be never a horse left ...'

'I know it. Best admit it do seem a most quick and awful sort of the disease – the farcy buds so big, and come to bursting or ever they was truly seen.'

'What shall we do that's best?'

'Be strong, for a start,' said Piers, shocked and dismayed by Harry's despair, that seemed so alien to his nature. 'God helping, it need not come to the worst.'

Harry did not answer. *The worst* should not be put into words, for they were stricken with a disease for which no cure was known – one which could be shared as fatally by man.

The Mantlemass manor secretary, Susannah reminded Judith, was as good as any apothecary – should she not fetch him to Cecilia?'

'Truly he is growing old – but he forgets nothing. I

know that, who am still his pupil. Richard knows it, too. Shall I find him, Judith?'

Cecilia was lying back against Judith's shoulder with her eyes closed, her head lolling. Her tears were finished, but she was breathing very heavily. Judith looked up at Susannah, frowning and anxious.

'She go over so fast, Susannah. I never saw such. Noontime, I thought I saw her bettering. Now it seem rushing on her. The fever's very high.'

'I'll fetch Master Woodward.'

But Judith checked her. She gathered Cecilia closer, as if to warm her, and told Susannah she should first go and tell the maids to bring more covers, and to heat and wrap bricks for the child's feet. The fever could only be sweated out, and the sooner the process was started the better in every way.

'How shall I keep Anne from her now? Yet now's the most needy time to stay away.'

As she spoke, Harry came in. Susannah said quickly, 'Cecilia's less well, cousin. I'll fetch Austin Woodward from Mantlemass – you know he has a rare hand in sickness.'

She ran from the room, unable to bear the sight of Harry's face, yet with no knowledge of how much he knew that those indoors had yet to learn. After she had seen the maids go running about her bidding, Susannah took up her cloak and ran out into the rain. Master Medley was crossing the yard and called out to her, to know where she was going, to tell her to wait ... Again she said she was to fetch Austin Woodward, to see if he could help Cecilia.

'Have you been with her?'

'Yes, sir. She is very sick.'

'You shall not go home today, then, Susannah.'

'Sir ...?'

'Better you stay, my maid. .We all must do what is best.

We must be wise, now, and work each for the other. Until the danger passes.'

'The danger ...' Like Richard earlier, Susannah felt herself chill and shiver. Perhaps she had never seen Medley so quiet and solemn, and because of it her mind raced to what was always the most feared. She smothered her dread and said firmly and clearly, 'Is it the plague?'

'Not as you think of it. Yet one way, t'other way, it may bring us all near death – or beyond.'

At this instant Harry ran out of the house, crying, 'Send for the priest! Father – the child's dying! Send Colin for Father Oswald. I must call Anne. Poor Anne – poor Anne – Judith has kept her from Cecilia! The shock could make her mad!'

'Come indoors,' his father said, catching Harry's arm. 'There are things to be said.'

'First send for the priest ... Susannah – you go to Anne. Tell her quickly, quickly!'

'No!' Master Medley said, thrusting Harry back towards the house. 'No, Susannah.'

Harry began to struggle with his father, striking out at him in black hatred, cursing him. Since Harry was now, by the passage of time, the stronger man, he broke from Medley eventually ... He started across the hall to the stairway door that led to the upper rooms where Anne had stayed all this time with the other children. Medley had been sent back against the wall by Harry's violence, but Susannah ran after him, ready to fight and drag him back by any foul means – since what Master Medley said must by all the laws known to them have sense and strength and reason.

But at the narrow door, with his hand on the latch, Harry checked – as if he too had recalled this tried truth. When he turned back to them, though he was white with the effort of controlling his despair, the wildness had left him.

'I understand,' he said. 'I do understand. I know what you are saying, sir.'

'We must work now to save what we may,' his father said. 'We must pray and we must work. Otherly, we shall all perish.'

Before this, Harry had admired his father's sudden strength that could rise and command them all. So now, as he decreed for every soul dwelling within the Ghylls Hatch boundary a new and rigid rule of life, there was no single dissenting voice. Men and maids, masters and servants, the old and the young, accepted and set about it.

Thus by courage, by wisdom and necessity, the entire establishment was divided. It was divided according to the order that once before had been invoked for salvation. Years ago, in the days of Roger Orlebar's father, the same disease had called for the same methods, and Medley had not forgotten being told the tale. Thus Master Medley and his sons kept themselves to the hall. Anne, deprived by now even of the comfort and relief of weeping, remained above as before. Judith and Susannah, with Nan and Bess, remained with Cecilia, whose strength came and went, but whose end none there doubted. No man who had handled any horse was to leave the demesne, nor for that matter any other man whose work lay about the place.

Thrice daily Medley, with Harry and Piers and Richard, went a tour of the stables, inspecting every horse in company with Matthew Ade and Rafe. The rest of the men were no longer allowed in the stables, but spent their days in constant clearing and cleansing, sweeping away the muck that had been already shoved outside, sluicing and raking. On the same fire that had devoured Black Lady's sad carcass, all excrement was burnt. This would come hard later when they needed manure for their fields, but instinct rather than any scanty knowledge told them that it was wise. They had little past experience, having been so fortunate in the health of their stock. Farcy came from poor conditions, anyone knew that. It came to animals shipped overseas for battle, crowded for long periods in stinking holds. Once introduced into a stable, as it had been here, it might in better circumstances have been checked. But the weather had been against them. So now every horse was each day walked in the yards, but not let into the fields where infection might linger. This was in itself an exhausting exercise for those who undertook it. Weariness increased daily, not helped by a time of year at which provisions were bound to be running low – as was feed for the horses.

It had been only on the last day of her life that Lady displayed the more common signs of farcy – the gummy nostril, the patched and pustulated skin, the swollen neck; but the disease must have been long dormant, since when they opened the cauterized place on her foreleg, it burst forth abominably. The Ottoman, as Piers had called him, must surely have dosed her with a sorcerer's magic that she had seemed so upstanding and blithe. Perhaps even before he set out to sell her at great profit on these shores, he had known of the trouble and had hastened to rid himself of the burden within a few miles of his place of landing. It was not the first time, certainly, that such a mountebank had spread sickness by the sale of an animal – a monkey, perhaps, a parrot, each with its own exotic charm that was so hard to resist ... There was no profit in speculation. By bad fortune and some lack of sense, they were left with a form of the disease particularly swift and violent – more savage in its impact than any account any one of them had ever heard.

Four days after Lady, they slaughtered Merope, Emperor, Brutus. A week after that went Richard's Breeze. On that day Cecilia, who had lain motionless and barely breathing three days and nights past, turned her head sideways and was still. There was no priest, no holy unction, no comfort for any soul under that roof.

'What have we done to her poor soul?' said Harry. 'I could have fetched Father Oswald here myself – but I obeyed you. How shall we be forgiven?'

'God shall judge me in this, not you,' Medley answered. 'He, too, is a father, and knows all our trouble.'

'What shall Anne say to me, then? How shall she forgive me?'

'She's stronger than you know. Else she'd have risked the rest for the sake of the one.'

That night, knowing it best done soon, they buried the dead child. Medley ordered a heap of brushwood set above the closed grave, and they fired it and stood watching until all was dark and ashes. The last smoke wisped upward and seemed to Harry, made fanciful by his misery, to carry away all that was left of his lovely daughter. He stood after the others had moved away, and seemed still to see a wraith of paler air curling against a sky swollen with rain. Strangely, the fire had comforted him. It was an element of the forest, where it swept often, destroying but cleansing, and then renewing. Out of its desolation there came fresh life, created out of destruction. It was his phoenix over again, and he lingered with the idea, glad of its promise. Then he seemed almost to hold the fire in his hand, miraculously contained – a gage to be flung down, a challenge to be hurled at some hour he could not number, for some purpose to which he could give no name . . .

At last, hardly able to drag his feet from one pace to the next, Harry went back to the house. In the hall the rest had withdrawn to the solitude of their grief, and in the rooms beyond there was a great silence. He stood a moment, unable to resolve his impulses. Then he crossed the hall. The little door that opened on the solar stairway was at the far corner, and he went to it, and pulled the latch, and stood in the opening. The stair wound its familiar way and at the top a lamp stood burning as always, faintly illuminating the steps.

He saw Anne sitting on the top step, very still, her knees drawn up to her chin, her hands over her head. Harry stood frozen, his longing so intense it made him groan softly, so that Anne raised her head.

'Harry . . .?'

He put his foot on the first stair, but she rose at once, almost fell in her haste, then ran out of sight. He heard a door close and a bolt shoot home.

He closed the stair-door and went back into the hall. He lay down near Richard and tried to sleep.

9

Siege

On the day the sickness was discovered, his father had sent Richard on foot to Mantlemass. When he reached the boundary he stood and shouted, and at last a man appeared who had been cutting rushes where the water spread out into a marshy stretch, growing the best rush and reed for miles around.

'Go ask my uncle come speak wi' me here,' Richard ordered. 'Say it's life or death and I dare not come nearer.'

The man ran off and Richard stood waiting for what seemed a dreary time. He imagined Simon Mallory arguing and disbelieving. But at last he came striding rather angrily down to the pinnold that crossed the river here. He was a tall strong man, grey-haired and bearded, practical and convinced in advance that there could be no reason on earth for him to go to Richard Medley, rather than Richard going to him.

Richard called out to him to keep his distance; and at that he did pause, puzzled and frowning.

'Richard? What's amiss?'

So then Richard told the tale of the sickness, of the toy horse destroyed and Cecilia near to death; how his father had decreed a strict way of life, none leaving Ghylls Hatch till danger was past, for fear of spreading the trouble about the forest; how even within doors they were to live separate. And for this reason Susannah, who had been close with Cecilia before the truth was known, must remain from home, for the sake of all there.

It had not been easy at first to convince his uncle, because he was so shocked and horrified at what he heard. He protested vigorously – he would have his daughter home, he would come himself to fetch her. But he had respected Medley for many years, though they had sparred as lads. In deep distress, he bowed to his cruel wisdom.

'Sir, my father said to recall for you what Master Roger Orlebar tell once – how the sickness struck but never spread about, and for this same reason – that they did all huddle and never stir abroad.'

'Many years gone, Richard. I misremember how the tale goes . . . But tell your father I accept his good sense.'

That was the last time anyone stepped beyond the Ghylls Hatch pale during the long weeks that followed. News came to Mantlemass only because Simon Mallory went daily to stand across the dick from Ghylls Hatch, and shout to one or other who looked out for him. The tidings he carried home were comfortless. When they heard of Cecilia's death, poor Mistress Mary grew frantic with grief and worry, begging that for Susannah the rule might be broken.

'Ride, husband – ride! Fetch her here to me fast! The trouble is theirs – are we to lose our daughter by their ordering?'

'It is for the best,' he said. 'My dear soul, try to understand.'

'The best? That Susannah should sicken?'

'Pray that she be saved,' he said patiently. 'You have a

better way of prayer than any of us under this roof. But if she be lost, then give thanks that two are left to us who might not be – save only for this cruel separation.' Her blotched and woeful face moved him to tenderness. 'Mary – understand what Anne Medley understands – that as many must be saved as may be, no matter how cruelly. Anne stayed from her daughter for hope that her sons should be saved.'

'She is hard, harsh – she is no mother . . .'

'She is strong,' he answered. 'God knoweth what it may cost her. When it is all over and we meet again, we need not look to meet the Anne we knew. That poor merry girl will be a woman full of wisdom most bitterly learned.'

Mary was silent a moment, then wept again. 'I have never been anyways wise or understanding,' she said; then leant against him for comfort which he tried hard to give, though he himself felt near despairing.

Dame Cecily had said they must have a sharp eye for their own horses, for until now there had been constant traffic between the two houses. There was no breeding done at Mantlemass, but they kept a large stable even through the winter. As at Ghylls Hatch every beast was inspected every day, so now at Mantlemass. On one day Simon would order the business, and the next it was his mother – it was her instinct for horses which had been handed down through her own daughter to her grandson, Piers. At Mantlemass, too, they used fires for cleansing – though the waste of dung, so necessary to cultivation, did rouse a protest in Simon, as well as in men who did the work.

'This must mean sad crops, mother. A year from now we might as good as starve.'

'God will see our trouble. He will know our good sense and he will help us.'

Simon did not answer this. A sceptical thread in his nature suggested that help was most needed now . . .

When Simon walked daily to Ghylls Hatch it was most often Susannah who stood across the stream and called the news to him.

'Child, are you well?'

'We are all well, sir. In the house all are well. Tell my mother so.'

'And all still living separate?'

'Aye – and that is a weary matter, surelye. But if none sicken indoors before the next moon, then Master Medley shall let the women and children be all together. But the men to stay separate from us – so long as any horse show sickness.

Some time later, a week or two it must have been, Simon knew the moment he saw his daughter that she had news.

'Is all well at Mantlemass, father?'

'Well enough. And here?'

'There is no sickness in the house . . .'

His spirits sank at the flatness in her voice. 'And in the stables?'

'There is a man ill, father . . .'

It was the middle of March, then, the disease still running, but the weather harder with some sun to cheer them. As bad fortune would have it, they were wintering more young stock than at any time they could recall. They had lost forty; ten more were in jeopardy. Royal Roan, the stallion whose well-being was all important, had quarters of his own far from the rest, even beyond the old stable where they had slaughtered Lady; Master Medley alone cared for him. When the man sickened, they had had a lull of more than a week, enough for cautious encouragement. Then Rafe, one near-noon, fell to the ground in some kind of spasm. They carried him to the barn, laid him on good straw, and covered him well. He came out of the rigor, but there were other signs.

Rafe was the son of Matthew Ade's sister, Dorcas Baldock, and it was Matthew who nursed him. On the third day of Rafe's illness, Matthew said that now he was bound to cross into the forest, for there was one sure way to save Rafe; which was by one of Peg Hoath's spells. Peg was related to Matthew from his mother's side and her reputation as a wise woman was very great in those parts. It was Harry who was consulted by Matthew, if consult was the word – like any other of these people, Matthew knew how to make up his own mind.

'I'll go b'night, sir, and none the wiser. Poor Rafe need help fast. Any know Peg's spells come mortacious powerful.'

Harry frowned. 'Wait, Matt. Speak first to my father.' He went in search of Master Medley and together they talked to Matt.

'What'd I say, Matt?' Medley reminded him. 'None to come and none to go. This we all kept to nobly – and see how rightly. Whatever come to us here, nor horse nor man over the forest took sick. You see that?'

'No priest, then, nor no portion neither,' said Matthew; not sullenly, for that was not in his nature, but bitterly disturbed. 'So how shall any be saved?'

'Rafe has medicines from the house,' Harry put in. 'You know Dame Judith is skilled in these things.'

'Not skilled enough to save the little maid, master,' said Matthew; then went red at saying it. 'I wonder the priest stay off from us. God could protect his own, surelye.'

'Master Mallory called news from Mantlemass,' Harry said, 'That Father Oswald got sent for to London and none see him since.' It had been his one consolation that it would in any case have been useless to go for the priest when Cecilia was dying. That, at least, was no longer on his conscience, though there was still enough.

Matthew stood shifting his feet a bit, seeming not to know where next to turn.

'We'm bound to face this, Matt,' Master Medley said, 'There's naun for any that takes the sickness – naun save death.'

'Peg Hoath cured Colin and Young Bunce,' Matthew said.

Harry looked sharply at his father. The two lads had complained of pains and sickness, and fear had made them worse. But they never had shown any true signs of farcy. Harry believed his father when he said that they had seen so much and thought so much that they had brought the feelings on themselves. Matthew's claim in these circumstances was upsetting and Harry thought his father lost colour a little.

'Now, Matt,' Medley said, 'how so? How did any come by spells or potions or advice from the wise woman – since none went from Ghylls Hatch into the forest?'

Matt said that Peg had a nose for profit, and had come to the boundary and waited there. He himself had seen her, and it was he who later collected what she left hidden in the dry ditch under the old pinnold that was now out of use.

'Bits o' cloth wi' threads pulled!' Medley cried contemptuously. 'Filthy grindings in powder – and stinkhorn water . . . I know well enough the kind of matter. There are noble herbs, fine simples and remedies from roots and such – but not these.'

'They were cured,' said Matthew. 'They are well now.'

'Never speak to me o' Colin and Young Walter Bunce!

They took the trouble in their minds – and by their minds it were banished. If faith in God may move mountains, then no doubt faith in Satan and his demons and their magical works may move a shiver o' fever.'

'Then,' said Matthew, 'should it not do so for Rafe?'

'I have said why not!'

Matthew said no more, only frowned, apparently accepting what he could not understand, as he had accepted all his life – as indeed they all accepted, reason being most often too weak for true comprehension.

'When Rafe die,' said Medley to Harry, 'as die he must, my good Matt will blame me.'

Harry did not say, for fear of angering his father, who was too hard pressed to bear much more, that Matt would not give up his idea of getting help from Peg. The forest nature was as unbending as the iron it throve on. For all that, Matt was a trusted and devoted servant, and Harry thought he would almost certainly get what he wanted without breaking the law laid down – he would not cross the pale.

Harry felt that his father had aged five years at least in these bitter days. Till now there had been no grey in his hair, but suddenly it had taken on a streaked and dusty appearance. Well, they had all aged, Harry knew. Each day he called up to Anne and she spoke to him from the window; if she smiled at all, it was the smile of a woman twice her age. Not only tragedy had aged her, but the physical strain of an intolerable way of life. In another day or two, Medley had promised, it must surely be safe for the women at least to be together. The men must remain as they were, since they were all the time handling the horses. The separated companies demanded much extra effort, and though they might be reduced from three to two, nothing could yet be easy. Tasks must fall still to

Anne, to Judith and Susannah which were out of their usual experience. Judith was no longer a young woman and the strain was showing in her, too, though Harry had only seen her fleetingly and at a distance. One night after dark she tripped over a stool, and grabbing at the settle back to save herself, fell awkwardly and broke a bone in her right wrist.

It was three days after this accident that the women were reunited. It was not an easy meeting, for they had done no more than call or wave to one another all this time. It was only now, in their reunion, that Cecilia's death seemed fully understood, and for Anne it was as though the child had died again. But the baby had grown and learnt how to smile, and there was much to be exclaimed over – this was a lustier boy than Jack had ever been, and so they could rejoice in him at least. For Harry, too, there was comfort in knowing that Anne's worst loneliness was over.

Because Anne was much occupied with the children, unable to bear them far from her, and Judith greatly hampered by her wrist, Susannah now became the one who controlled their household. Of them all, she was perhaps the most changed, coming to a situation of disaster and dread almost before her childhood was over; she would not be fifteen until the summer. Yet she accepted the task firmly and easily. As the days moved into spring, and the men of the household remained quartered in the hall, it was Susannah who supported the rest.

When Rafe died, the news went out into the forest as all other news had gone. His mother, Dorcas Baldock, with her two elder sons and her unmarried daughter, came to stand on the bank beyond the water, waiting there silently.

Rafe had been buried the night before, like Cecilia without any blessing, for there was still no word of the priest. Matt Ade came to call across to the mourners, shouting out the words because the water between them ran so fast after the recent sodden season.

'Sister,' Matt bellowed to Dorcas, 'it were the best got done for'm. He die peaceful. Dame Judith's medicines did soothe him, they give'm easy breathing.'

No one answered. They turned, the mother leaning on her sons, the daughter trailing behind, and went off slowly into the forest.

Some time later, Matt brought strange news to Harry.

'It were true, sir, Peg Hoath could do naun for Rafe. Reu Goodale called across this noon – Peg upped wi' her goods in a cart, and her goats following on, and went across the forest, eastward. I niver crossed out, but the spell got left for'm. There was no good in it.'

'I feared not. My father knew not,' Harry said.

'As well Peg left,' said Matt. 'They burnt down her place last night.'

Harry barely stopped himself thanking Matt for this news. It meant at least that the blame for Rafe's death had been placed, however unfairly, on the wise woman.

After Rafe, none sickened but the animals. The advancing spring blew a great gale from the south-west, huge clouds fled across the bright sky, but nothing brightened below. Of ten horses threatened a few weeks ago, seven had declined faster than any yet – among them Anne's loved Proserpine, that first gift from the days of her wooing. Also Verity went, of a line that was ending anyway, for it seemed now bred out, and there had been some surprise that she had withstood the sickness so long – her sister, Dignity, was an early victim. It now became best sense to slaughter any animal that showed positive signs, and so the remaining three of this batch were dealt with. Any thought the Medleys may have had at the outset that the disease, being different in some aspects from what they knew, might therefore also be cured, had long ago been forgotten. Of the stock remaining, some seemed in good heart, but others were in one manner or another diminished. Some weeks before this, Harry had declared they should dispatch every horse on their land and so dispose of the matter finally. But his father and brothers cried out against it. The very season could be the cause of some poorness – there was feed enough, since the demand was so much diminished, but the quality was miserable. Damp had got at the oats, the bran seemed ready to ferment. It was unfortunate that the chizzle, the bran, had been poorly milled – millers came and went, since mills were easily destroyed, and not all millers were skilful. Medley would have given much for good feed just then – he might almost have said that enough for one horse would do, for now all his hopes were on Royal Roan, stamping in his solitude and increasingly ill-tempered. From him they could begin again to build up Ghylls Hatch. In his care of this animal, Medley became a madman, letting none other near it, not even Piers, exhausting himself over its welfare.

The gale blew for three days and at its height was severe. Eight grown trees fell on Ghylls Hatch alone.

'There'll be n'beast n'timber left us, prensly,' Matt Ade said to Harry. 'God smite us.'

'He smite the whole forest, Matt. Look out and see how much come down. The stand of beech over along the Staglye track suffered worst.'

From Ghylls Hatch, the forest seemed full of gaps. When the wind died, men appeared on the tracks obstructed by fallen trunks and branches, with axes and saws and chains, to chop and shift and cart away the wood. Some did it fast enough to grab a supply for their own hearths, but the wood-reeve marked the rest for the King, as was the law. The rangers could be seen, then, lopping and chopping, while others looked on, resigned rather than resentful. They mostly stood in some sort of kinship, anyway, a situation with many advantages.

Harry and Piers had gone out to deal with a fallen beech that had crashed on the third night of the storm. They looked down the bank, and saw a dozen or more foresters busy about dealing with the woodfall. It was a long time since they had seen any but the one or two who came for news of their relatives working at Ghylls Hatch. Watching this everyday work of the forest, work that came out of the seasons' steady progression from end to end of the year, the brothers stood silent and still. Each was filled with an emotion he would have found impossible to express. It was the emotion of an exile, of a castaway who sees at last that what had seemed an alien or an empty world is still peopled and familiar. Rooted in their own disaster, Harry and Piers saw others still easy and unafflicted. The uprising of feeling resolved into a strange compound of envy and bitterness, yet of something also very near to love. Not a man there below but they could have called and greeted, asking by name after his wife, his children, his old mother, his lame sister . . .

At last Harry said, 'They all look hale, thank God.'

The stillness following in the wind's wake must have taken and tossed his voice, for one of the men paused in his work and looked up. Involuntarily, eagerly, Harry raised his hand in greeting.

The men – one of the younger Goodales, Amos – turned away after only a second, and went back to his work. But after a stroke or two of the axe, he paused. He spoke to one of his fellows, leaning towards him, just glancing back over his shoulder as he did so. Then another paused and spoke – that was Hal Urry, whose father, another Hal, had sat at lessons with Master Medley, and should have inherited a prosperous iron-working, only the family had mismanaged and fallen on hard times. All three men had their backs turned to the brothers, but again came the glance over the shoulder. Then one by one, and calling to others round about, the men swung their axes into the cart, tossed in what wood was handy, and moved away. It was that moment of the year when the birches, their catkins come near to bursting, carry about them a purple effulgence, almost a mist of colour, the promise of their coming maturity. The men moved into this mist and were curiously absorbed by it, so that within seconds they might never have been.

Piers said, 'They fear us. Harry! They fear us . . .'

For the first time since the tragedy had struck them, his firmness left him. He had been steady enough to surprise Harry, but now he went down on one knee as if he could not support the great weight of sadness and remorse. He pulled his cap off and hid his face in it.

Harry did not speak to him, but picked up his axe, weighed it and swung it against the fallen trunk. The white chips flew from under the great blade, and the sound of the blows, the thud of the axe on the wood that was so strong, yet not strong enough to resist destruction, sounded out hard and harsh over the forest. Increased by the wind that now tossed aside the stillness, rising again with the ending of the day, the heavy defiant sound chopped at the solitude. Birds flew upward sounding those cries which, like the birches, spoke of spring, of renewal, of all that should be fair and promising . . . For Harry it was as though he aimed his great blows against his own conscience, and it gave and shattered, too weak to stand against the onslaught of so much self-inflicted disaster. A resentment near to hatred filled him – against his father, against Piers and Richard, against the women of the household and the servants in the stable yards – not because they had blamed him, but because no word of blame had been spoken by any single soul from the very second when they knew certainly what they must deal with. Their forbearance, in this sour moment of his life, seemed only weakness, their silence all but scarcey-witted. It was necessary for his peace of mind that guilt should be admitted, no man had ever so fiercely desired to do penance; yet by sheer loving forbearance, Master Medley had denied his eldest son the relief of expiation.

And there was a double edge to Harry's remorse. Because of what had come to Ghylls Hatch on the day he bought the toy horse for Cecilia, and bought it through his own blind obstinacy, he knew they must find themselves without support. It would take many years to rebuild the stud and the flourishing trade that had made them, not rich, but settled. They must find other means, and there was only one other; the iron he so longed to work. They would come to it, will they, nil they, but there could be no triumph in it for him. It would be as if he had plotted the whole tragedy, destroying not only the work of generations, but killing his own loved daughter in the achievement of his ambition ...

This was reasoning past all reason but Harry was in fact a little out of his mind just then. He threw down the axe and shouted at Piers, 'Gird up, for Christ's sweet sake! Leave maundering over your misery and get to work. I'm spent. Take the axe! Take the axe, curse you – I've had enough!'

Piers swung the axe in his turn, hard and long, and after a bit Harry recovered some sense and began using the saw on the lopped branches.

They stayed working on the tree until the light went, with no word between them. At last Harry called a halt. They shouldered axe and saw and turned for home.

To the west of Ghylls Hatch, where the track took its turn towards Mantlemass, a second river ran along that pale and was crossed by a bridge wide enough to take a cart. Harry and Piers, their work done, were climbing in the dusk up the steep bank towards the house, with all its dependent buildings crowding about it in a great mass against the darkened sky; Mantlemass was away on their right. The sky growing swollen, as if blown up by the returning wind, the dark and the noise increased with every moment. They would have been unable to see anyone approaching their boundary, if it had not been for a lantern bobbing and swinging along, and its shed light just showed the unmistakable figure of Father Oswald. A second more, and they saw that he headed a straggling collection of about twenty men.

'Turn 'em off!' Harry cried to Piers. 'It'll send father out of his mind if they cross the water!'

At its nearer side, the bridge was obstructed, but only by a token cross of birchwood; no more was needed. Although it seemed unlikely that the priest would sweep aside such a barrier, any more than others had done, he was a man of great determination and might carry the rest with him. Harry therefore ran down in a long diagonal towards the advancing column, while Piers went further, to station himself if need be at the barrier. Both were aware that all the care of the last miserable weeks could be undone at a blow, and Harry was troubled besides, to realize that the priest might censure them for two unhallowed burials.

As Father Oswald reached the head of the bridge, Harry bellowed out to him to stop. He did so instantly, checking those behind him – but they, in any case, hung back. The priest held up the lantern, hoping to see who called, but its small ray did not greatly help him.

'Harry Medley, Father!' Harry shouted, coming as near as seemed sensible. 'Best not come closer.'

'Harry, Harry!' cried the priest. 'I am barely returned to Staglye. I was sent for to London – I knew nothing of your woes. What could you think of me, that I was all this time away?'

Sent for to London surely meant that he too, poor man, had had his woes.

'Is all well with you, Father Oswald?'

'Well enough ... Let that be how't will. I am home ... But you are sorely tried, my son.'

'Aye,' said Harry shortly. He looked past the priest at the shadowy crowd in the background. 'You have others with you. An army ...'

By now Piers had moved nearer, and Harry was glad of it, feeling he might need support.

'I came to Staglye only at noon, Harry. They brought me the news. They are greatly troubled ... Let me come closer.'

'You may not cross the pinnold,' Piers called to him. 'My father made this law. For the good of all.'

'Yes, my son, yes. It is marked and accepted. But they say more could be done.'

'What more? The sickness is checked.'

'I thank God for it, as you do. But they fear there may yet be means of its spreading.'

'What more are we to do for 'em? As the horses sicken,

so they are slaughtered. Of the – the two human victims – both are safe buried. All this is well known.'

'The wind blows so long and strong from the south – this greatly disturbs them. They know well such winds are not healthy.'

Piers shouted out in his turn, losing his temper at this insistence. 'If it blow *from* the south, it blow *to* the north, surelye. It take a chucklehead to think otherly!'

'These people live north of Ghylls Hatch.'

Now they all began to shout. The wind was indeed in a tumult once again, and the row of it in the trees, and the piercing sound of it gashing its way along the bottoms like a flood, with the dark now fluctuating to a full moon that was hurled from cloud to cloud, and with the lantern beginning to splutter and dim, made such madness of the scene it was barely tolerable. Least of all might any Medley, or any Mallory, accept it, after the long years of quiet living among people so well known and understood, with a trust on both sides that was near to loving.

Behind him, Harry heard a crashing stride he knew must be his father's. He was at once relieved and filled with dread of what Medley might say; for he was further stretched than any of them, a man on a rack inexorably turned and tightened.

'Is that you, Harry? Piers? What now?'

'It is the priest, sir. Father Oswald's returned to us – and brings others with him out of the forest. For they are anxious, he say.'

'What do they want? I cannot see you clear, Father Oswald. No! Come no closer. I have my hearing, as you have. Tell me what they want.'

His voice coming through the gloom was immeasurably commanding, his speech very clear; as always at such times it was divested of all foresty inflections.

'I ache with shouting,' the priest said. 'My trust is in God. I must come nearer.'

But at that the foresters protested furiously, pulling and plucking at him so that he was forced to fall back.

'Master Medley! Master Medley!' he cried, very hoarse indeed. 'They say there is more to do. They speak of the way it went for the Orlebars.'

There was a second's total silence while Medley swallowed this. His sons waited for his anger to burst out, but he was quiet.

'What more?' he asked.

'They say – and how am I to know either way – they say there are sick animals you will not destroy.'

There was the merest pause, then Medley said, 'Tell them we have lost all but a handful. But they stay healthy.'

Someone shouted out, 'No! No!' and there was a lot of talk and some shouting, yet still there seemed somehow no malice in it, only anxiety. They could not really know, these outsiders, how things stood at Ghylls Hatch – it was only their instinctive knowledge of natural things that told them what should be done. It was knowledge shared by Medley and the rest, but they believed they had progressed. The stark good sense of the foresters told them that until all was destroyed the disease could strike again. It was from this point that Medley believed he had progressed – his instinct was rather to save what could be saved, even at the heart of the area that was so cursed.

He called out to them asking them to understand. 'There's been no sickness for a week past. If we must live separate a year and more – if we come to starvation – yet we'll save some. If we cannot – then Ghylls Hatch is done for.'

In the crowd, someone then called out a name – Royal Roan – and Harry heard himself groan in protest. If there was to be a future, then it lay with Royal Roan.

'He's whole and well,' Medley had answered.

'Breed him agin – you breed death agin! You dursen't, master! Never breed death or death'll sure do for all! B'now the ground's sick – the grass never feed any but corpses!'

Medley said shortly, his voice roughing in defeat, 'Take 'em away, Father Oswald. I've nothing to say more to them now.'

He turned and began striding away. No one called out after him. The encounter ended in silence. Once again, a cluster of men disappeared into their background. The wind, the night, the hurrying moon, took over the forest.

Harry and Piers waited a little, then they followed their father back to the house. Neither spoke on the way, but each was occupied with the same uneasy thought. They had been threatened all this time by powers too great to be named, yet they had at least contained disaster. Now they were threatened from outside.

In the courtyard, Richard was talking to Matthew Ade and Young Walter Bunce. He ran forward when he saw his father. Walking heavily and slowly, his striding done and defeated, Medley was by now no more than a few paces ahead of Piers and Harry.

'Well?' he said, as Richard came to him in the half-light of the door cressets. 'Is it horse or human?'

'Horse, sir.'

'I thank God for it.'

'The worst yet . . .' Richard said.

'Then it is the stallion. It is what they feel they need. The end of Ghylls Hatch.'

10

Foresters' Law

'Let me be – I dare not speak of it – I dare not think of it,' Master Medley had said. And thereafter he had gone indoors and sat silent and withdrawn from all of them. He badly needed Judith to comfort and counsel him over the bitter news of Royal Roan.

Sometime in the first hours of the morning, when all weary souls should have been sleeping, Harry woke. He heard his father speaking quietly to Piers, who was lying nearest to him. He was speaking of the Orlebars, who had come to Ghylls Hatch somewhere in the middle years of the past century.

'It were Roger Orlebar I knew – his father being a long time dead. When he died was at the time this same trouble struck them. They had fifty horses b'then, the stud just building well again after all the trouble wi' York and Lancaster. That's a thing we know naun of in our time – as yet; the horses'd be seized and rid away by one side, t'other side, it made no matter ... It was the Orlebars' great horses had all the fame – for battle and for jousting.' He was silent, thinking of that time as it had been related to him, of that disaster so like their own, yet less in number, less in the span that had gone to making Ghylls Hatch what it now was; and less in that there had been no human sickness. 'His heart broke,' Medley said. 'Old Orlebar – though he were not old in years. His heart just cracked apart. He died in the twelvemonth.'

Again he was silent, then spoke again, his voice now very gentle. 'Master Roger Orlebar brought me to all I ever had ... And he gave me my first pair o' boots for riding. Because I pleased him some way I rode a horse of his ... He was a good and loving man, God rest his soul.'

Harry heard Piers saying something. The moonlight was striking in and lying about the floor, and Harry saw that Piers had reached out his hand and laid it on his father's arm, and that Medley in turn had clasped it there, accepting the comfort. It was a gesture that Harry himself could never have made – he felt his father's misery as deep as any could, he would have given much for Piers's easy warmth.

'What did they save of their stock?' Piers asked.

'Nothing.'

After a moment, Piers recovered from this and said that Echo, of the brood mares, still seemed hearty. 'And in foal to Royal Roan. She'd be our roots and our new start here.'

'The Orlebars saved no stock because they were bolder, Piers. So should I ha' bin. I never spoke this to any but you, and maybe I'll not speak it again – save in the confessional. They saved themselves and their men and all about in the forest and checked the sickness where it began. They were bolder and braver than your father bin.'

'There were fewer horses ...'

'All were destroyed in the first seven days. All. There were certain to be some about the forest who'd remember. They'll not rest easy till all's done here the same – the pasture burnt off and ploughed and marled. I know this from the start. Only it come hard – too hard.' He pulled up his cloak and turned his shoulder. 'Get back to sleep, boy,' he said.

The hall was silent, then, and it seemed they all slept, some deeper than others – Richard often cried out and muttered. Harry, too, dozed uneasily, constantly starting awake and peering round, as if knowing there must be more to the night than mere sleep and wretchedness. They had gone over a week this time without any further sign of sickness, giving them all hope that they dared not speak out loud. Reunion had seemed nearer, but now they must wait again. The separation was a sickness in itself. Its greatest pain for Harry was in not knowing whether Anne blamed him for their daughter's death. Would she ever be able to tell him, even in the most secret moment, or must it lie between them for ever? Would she be strong enough to forgive him his fault in judgement, as his father and his brothers were; and even the men working in the place?

An hour, maybe, after Medley had been talking to Piers, Harry woke again and saw his father leaving the hall by the main door. Piers and Richard were sleeping deeply now. Harry got up and pulled on his boots. He followed his father out into the chill early morning. In the way of such weather it had stilled and quieted, the wind forgotten, the sky clear. The moon, now on the point of setting, seemed to hang barely above the treetops. Over by the barns and the granary, the dogs barked, rattling against the doors where they had been too long confined. Medley would have passed that way, bound most certainly for Royal Roan's distant stable.

Harry followed cautiously. He wanted nothing so much as to help his father over the next appalling task. He might not be able, like Piers, to express his feelings by word or touch, but he could offer some practical assistance. He moved free of the outbuildings, with their long moon-drawn shadows – then he was facing out over the forest where the Ghylls Hatch land ended at its enclosing line of water.

He saw what stopped him hard in his tracks. He actually stumbled in his amazement and shock.

There was a fire burning on the far bank, a hundred or so paces up from the bottom, close by a track that ran off among scrub to the stand of beech at the summit. Having taken in one fire, Harry saw that there were others. They were drawn in an encircling line as far as he could see in either direction. He knew instantly that there would be others that the rise in the land concealed . . .

Harry thought of the moat at Easingwell, that had been dug and maintained to keep men out. These fires had been lit to keep men in. The foresters had laid siege to Ghylls Hatch.

There was some slight sound behind, and Harry swung round, nervous and edgy. But it was only Piers, who had missed his father and came hurrying, lacing his jerkin as he came, with Richard behind him, half asleep and stumbling.

'Look here, Piers,' Harry said. 'Richard – look.'

The three brothers stood together and stared towards the fires. There was a dark movement across the flame from time to time. As fresh fuel was thrown on, the flames leapt, the light increased, they could see the men tending the fires.

'We bin a long while in this country,' Richard said. 'I reckon they could'a trusted more.'

'Fear make men mad,' Piers answered him. 'Fear goes over, one way, t'other way. Trust come back agin . . . And this'll make our father mad, too, seems me. Best find him.'

They went at once along the path running by Horndown, where Harry had watched Cecilia joyfully cantering her toy horse, and came to the farthest building of all, where Medley had taken the stallion at the first onset of trouble, and tended him so jealously ever since. They saw their father standing by the open stable door, but he was not alone – Matt Ade was with him.

Piers said, with such relief in his voice as seemed hardly to match the moment, 'Matt done it for him! God bless him – for I do bluv my father'd near as soon've killed himself.'

He ran forward, and Richard with him; Matt looked round at them, his face strangely marked with sadness and shame at what he had done for the best. Only Harry remained a moment behind the rest, struggling with thoughts that would not be contained, but raced and whirled. Then he, too, went towards Medley, trying as he went to rouse up words that would match so hard a moment.

Medley seemed glad to see him – glad of the chance to shift and speak and get the rest of the business over.

'The stallion's gone,' he said. 'So there we stand. Soon we'll be left wi' naun but our own wits – and mine feel in a fair shatter now.' He spoke quite strongly, as a man is often able to at the worst moment, to sorrow later.

'Come back, sir,' Harry said. 'Get back to sleep.'

'Sleep?'

Harry felt himself redden and was glad there was so little light. 'Some rest,' he corrected himself.

'Work to do. Best it get done before light.' He straightened his shoulders, saying almost aggressively, 'There's four left, as I reckon.'

There was Psyche and Agate, Garnet, who was the fifth of that name, and Echo – save Garnet, all mares, with

Echo marked for a fine brood. At Echo's name, Master Medley did pause and look at Piers, then went on rapidly to plan her destruction.

'Four o' them and four to deal with 'em,' he said. 'Matt – take Agate; Piers, Garnet; Richard, Psyche. I'll take my turn with Echo.'

'That's for me,' Harry said. 'Matt save you the stallion's death – then I'll save you Echo's.'

Medley shook his head. 'Not you, Harry. Ask Piers why. I'm in no shape to fumble over excuses.'

Harry looked sharply at his brother. 'Well?'

'A man needs love a horse to kill it clean. No more offence than that, Harry.'

The fires that ringed Ghylls Hatch were matched and surpassed that night and the next day, and the next, by those within the boundary. Once again, the smell of consuming horseflesh, of hair and bone, hung in a cloud, then drifted on the soft breeze that had followed the gale, far out over the forest. The sun came out that day, making the fires look pale. Primroses opened, birds flew with twigs and straw. The forest stirred, the season grew. The deer moved in the deep glades and the does in fallow clustered together.

When the last bone, the last hoof and horn of the Ghylls Hatch sacrifice was consumed, terrible exhaustion lay over the place. Beyond the pale, the fires were still tended; in spite of the slaughter, the watchers did not move away. As Medley had known, there was more to do. The ground must be scoured and purified. It was a large area, and being so much kept for grazing, offered little hold for burning. For a day or two following that final holocaust, no plan could be made. The wits of every man there were used up, tired out through dealing with an ever-mounting disaster, with the sudden collapse of the imposed rule of life that had kept them all this time at fever pitch. The physical strength went out of them. The stable men hung about idle and weary; the farrier and the smith leant yawning by the cold anvil; and within doors the mood was the same. There was a silence from the women's quarters, the children were hushed. A world had ended.

And while all three brothers watched their father, waiting for him to rouse up and order what must be done next, so Richard watched Harry and Piers in turn; he frowned over thoughts of a future which, for Piers, seemed hardly to exist, for Harry might mean at last that new life he had yearned after for so long. And for Richard himself – what? It was a query he hardly dared put into shape. He fumbled over it and knew no solution. Piers he loved best, but since his own sorrows Piers had lacked purpose. Yet it seemed to Richard hard to believe that the future lay with Harry.

After three days, Medley picked himself up. He collected the remnants of his authority and decided how best to order what was left of life as they knew it.

'Much to be done,' he said, 'and none but us shall do it. Therefore it seems best to me that the wives and the children, and Susannah, shall be sent now to Mantlemass. Best Susannah go first and speak with her father and with Dame Cecily. For it must be there we get our Yea or Nay.' He looked at Harry's black face. 'Be patient.'

'I have been.'

'It need not be long now. Never throw all away that we endured together, Harry. Never leave till all's done.'

'No, sir,' said Harry; but coldly, thinking: *There speaks an old man . . .*

Later, they stood at a distance to watch Susannah on her way to Mantlemass. Judith had come to the window, as she had done every day of the long weeks, and Medley had told her what was decided.

'Are the fires out, husband?'

'No, my dear soul. Not yet. Not yet . . .'

Susannah was excited to be going home. She looked for Richard and smiled across at him, but the weeks of strain were clear in her face and she had somehow a dusty and neglected appearance – like a cloak that has hung too long on the same peg.

'Greet Dame Cecily for me, and your good mother,' Medley called to her. 'Say how we pray to be all together again.'

Susannah nodded only, and ran off down the path to the gate and the bridge over the little river. Richard followed her down, but keeping his distance. Once or twice she looked back over her shoulder. The light behind him made Richard look taller, and beyond him, by now on the horizon, Master Medley, and Harry, and Piers, appeared like giants. Ahead she saw the fires, with their patient, persistent attendants. She wondered, as the others were wondering for her, what greeting she might receive when she reached them . . .

As she approached, a man who had just thrown wood on the fire, stepped a little forward and then stood his ground. He spoke and Susannah answered, but it was not possible for the watchers to hear what was said.

'That's Walter Penfold,' Piers said. 'Young Walter, that is. Rest easy, Dickory. He's a suent, smiling lad.'

He was smiling now. He stepped back, almost with a bow, and Susannah went on her way, her back rather stiff. The lad watched her go, and when, farther up the track, she turned and waved to Richard, Walter took the salutation to himself and waved back.

'All's well,' said Piers. 'That's one worry the less.'

The brothers smiled, one to another, and it seemed as though their faces had been stiff and unmoved for a very long time. There was some loosening, then, of all their muscles, and as they walked back with their father, they were talking together in a free and reasonable manner. When Susannah passed the fire and sped on her way to Mantlemass, one part of life, at the least, had begun again.

Later that day, Susannah returned, bringing her father and five or six of the Mantlemass men, but all on foot. The men at the fires watched but made no move. Two of the Mantlemass servants, Greg Henty and his young brother, hesitated to cross the pinnold on to Ghylls Hatch land, and this was respected. The others were easy and trusting. Simon went with Susannah as far as the house, then waited as she said he should, at the little door that led to the rooms away from the hall. Almost immediately, Judith came out, her hand and wrist swathed, and looking very pale and drawn. Then Anne came, holding Jack by the hand, and Bess carrying Lewis, and Catherine with Susannah. Nan and the other women servants followed, and the men who had come from Mantlemass shouldered the various bundles they brought with them. Simon helped Judith down the steep path, encouraging her, telling her that now all would soon be well. At the gate, Judith paused and looked back. The Medleys had kept away. There was no soul in sight. The house stood gauntly, abandoned by those who cared best for it and so gave it warmth and comfortable shelter for the rest.

'Husband ...' said Judith, in a low, sad voice. For the first time in all the weeks and months, she wept.

They crossed the bridge and went on up the track, and since old Goody Penfold was among the Ghylls Hatch servants, she scolded her grandson tending the fire, and shook her fist at him as she passed. The strange procession straggled on up the rough track, winding eventually out of sight of Ghylls Hatch, but coming then to the welcome and security of Mantlemass.

Now came, in terms of labour, the hardest time of all. By now every Ghylls Hatch man knew that the besieging fires would not be allowed to die until all was done that must be done. There was no enmity in it, only hard reasoning and curiously, trust. The trust had been shown when they let the women through, confident that if he had not believed it safe, Master Medley would not have sent them to Mantlemass. But further they would not go. When all was done – then only would the siege be lifted and the stubbornly watchful foresters return to sleep under their own roofs at night.

Therefore the stables and the barns and stores, the fields and paddocks, the entire ground that was Ghylls Hatch ground – save only that part west and a little southward of the house, where no horse ever passed, and where none tending them had walked, leaving that place for the women – all this must be cleansed to the bone and beyond. On the day after the women had left for Mantlemass, the task was begun.

First the ground was strewed with litter from the great store that had been cut as usual at the fall of the previous year. There was much of it, since the horses it was intended for had grown fewer and fewer as the winter went on. The fields were squared off and worked piece by piece. The litter was fired, and gradually the grass began to smoulder and the fire to creep. In midway areas, between field and field, where bramble and gorse had marked the boundaries, the burning was in one way easier – the bushes were faster igniting, the gorse flared and spat, the bramble roared; but the land was spronky – that is, full of old roots and stools of birch and even oak, that had been cut and cut again without systematic coppicing, merely for the sake of convenience. The hollards resisted the flames with such gallantry that many had to be reduced to charcoal and then broken down before they were totally destroyed. The weather at least was dry, there was a fairish wind to help them along, though they might have done better with the gales that had blown a week or two back. There were twenty men in all, including the two kitchen boys left behind when the rest of the household went to Mantlemass; the master and his sons worked alongside the rest, hour for hour, burden for burden.

In the first two weeks, they burnt off seven-eighths of the land; in the third they were checked for the first time by rain. It was light, but persistent, too persistent for firing open ground. So, in the lull, they turned to the stables. There was some question as to how this would be best done, but in the end they did the obvious, firing the thatches and burning the lot to the ground. Wooden stalls, wooden mangers, straw in the lofts, made quickish work of all this; but walls would still remain, and these they fell upon with picks and axes and hewed them down. The destruction was so immense, it needed such strength, that it began to move to a rhythm, and they none of them thought any longer of what it meant, why they were doing it – their sole concern became the speed with which they worked, the efficiency they could display. Once the litter was used up they would be bound to cut much young timber on their own ground, or the burning would never be completed. The bracken at this time of the year still lay in dry russet swathes over the forest floor, but beyond the Ghylls Hatch boundary.

Matt looked over at the far slopes and the men who kept the fires.

'There's what we need, master.'

'There's what we dare not take, Matt. Till all's done they think on us as sick horses ready to trample 'em.'

'Yet I do reckon we'm fairly pickled and smoked dry b'now,' Matt answered.

They both laughed. Richard, working near by, looked up in astonishment.

'Matt say we'm all smoked like hanging hams, Dickory!'

Richard laughed in his turn – not entirely to please them, but because it did seem a goodish joke, things being what they were.

The next day, or maybe the next, they were all much alike, there was some coming and going among the tenders of the perpetual fires. They began scything the remaining bracken, piling it at the crossings of the narrow river. At first there was much alarm at this, for it was feared the foresters meant to destroy the pale. Master Medley called to the cutters.

'What now? We done our best and near done all.'

It was Amos Goodale he spoke to. 'Master,' said Amos, 'we see you and yours fair jawled out wi' work and care. More litter's needed for burning off the rest. We'd as well do some cutting, better'n stand nabbling all the day.'

After that, they cut each day. The Ghylls Hatch men carried the litter and spread and burnt the remaining ground. Then they set to ploughing. The black sods turned before the plough's blade, curling into furrows that were then ploughed cross-wise. It was killing work; for the ploughing was done in the old manner – not with horses, nor with oxen, but by men unaided.

Suddenly there was no more to be done. One moment the work seemed still in full swing – then there was no more. Even the smoke that had rolled so long over Ghylls

Hatch, thinned and fanned and was blown away in pale strands. But a haze remained over all, as if the fire lay breathing.

Exhausted as they were, all were in good health. That evening Medley called his men into the hall, and they broached the last of the ale that was left of the winter's store, and cut down the last ham. The kitchen boys knew how to bake, so there was bread, though the flour remaining in the bottoms of the bins made a sour and heavy dough. Yet this seemed a feast beyond all feasts, and most drank more than they needed, many dropping to the floor and sleeping noisily where they fell. There was neither profit nor gratitude in reproaching them.

'Tomorrow, Richard,' his father said, and his own speech could have been clearer, 'tomorrow get you to Mantlemass. Tell your grandmother we are done at last, that under God we believe ourselves clean. Ask her, may we come to Mantlemass, and rest there a little.'

Then they all slept. It was strange to reach contentment through so much destruction and desolation, yet they did feel content. The dark night sealed them in their exhausted satisfaction as if they had been lovers, not butchers, of all but a century's work and hope.

Harry woke with Piers shaking him by the shoulder. It was still dark, and he groaned.

'Quiet!'

'What . . .?' Harry mumbled. 'What now –?'

'Harry – Harry, listen. I have been outside . . .'

'Not the only one, I'd say . . . Too much ale . . .'

'Wake up. Wake up and come outside with me.'

'I know what I'll see – Nothing! Nothing and nothingness to all eternity!'

'Do's I say, brother.'

Piers spoke very quietly, close to Harry's ear. There was great urgency in his quiet voice, and he was cold sober, as Harry was not altogether. He struggled up, Piers hauling him with a hand under the armpit, then stumbled outside.

In spite of the moon being dark, the sky held some light; enough to show how strangely the outlook was changed. Unbroken now by the sharp angles of wall and roof that had stood sheltering the house from the open weather, it seemed from the fall of the ground towards the water that nothing held them from the open pit of the sky.

'We done well, ask me,' said Harry, slurring into the old forest rhythms.

'Not well enough, maybe.'

Then Harry was sober, as if he had plunged his head into cold water.

'Piers . . .?'

'The fires are still bright, Harry. The siege seem no way raised. So, then – there's more needs be done.'

'What *more*? There's nothing left!'

But he knew. He knew even before he saw that while they celebrated their release from labour, men had come from the forest with great piles of young timber, of brushwood, of the last of the brakes. There were mounds and heaps of it spread on the untouched ground to the west, where at last the foresters had stepped, admitting it to be clean. The biggest pile of all was set over against the far wall of the house, with beside it a small fire that was smouldering now, but its message as clear as if were spelt with a stick in the ashes.

'They want the house down, Harry. They want that, along wi' all the rest.'

'Ah, then,' said Harry, his anger rising, 'there's a thing they cannot have, surelye!'

'You tell them so, brother,' Piers said.

11

The Siege Raised

'What man ever took orders to burn down his own house?' Master Medley cried. 'Nor'll I be the first!' His roused anger pleased Harry, troubled Piers – and to Richard's younger ears sounded a note that was slightly false. 'There was the child sick indoors,' Medley insisted, as if convincing himself, 'but none other, nor any sign or sound of sickness more.'

Piers said, 'But we, all-us, come to the hall and dwell there, sir. And each day, all day we did work wi' the poor beasts.'

'Then the hall shall be scoured.'

'I doubt that satisfy, father,' Piers said.

'Richard,' his father said, 'get to Mantlemass. Tell what's afoot and ask they send help. Maybe your uncle shall show them sense. Or better than any – your grandmother. She've a fine sharp tongue, come she choose so.'

Richard went off as he was bidden, but he was back in five minutes.

'I'm not let through. Not, they say, till all – all – be safe and seared.'

'They're half on 'em my tenantry!' Medley shouted. 'Shall they tell me what's to do?' He looked round him at his own men, who had stood by him and toiled with him and now needed rest and a fresh start to life. 'Then we all go to Mantlemass. Let 'em stop us if they may.'

He strode off without any time for reflection, for preparation, empty-handed and vigorous, as though he had never known the meaning of weariness and despair. Behind him came first Harry, then Piers and Richard – Richard slipping back into his childhood's habit of hunching up his shoulders in excitement so that both might look level. Then came the men, in no particular order, but more or less under the eye of Walter Ade and the older Bunce: the farrier, the smith; the saddler, fourth generation of the Awcock family who had worked for the Orlebars; then a shatter of stablemen and grooms, among them Colin Crutten, Ben Grover; and last the two kitchen boys, Tom Godsmark and Dick Bostel. Dick was a distant relative of Judith Medley, and Tom of her first husband, and whether either lad would settle to the kitchen again seemed open to considerable doubt; the hard work had made them both grow, Dick's jerkin had burst across the shoulders, and Tom went barefoot because he had grown out of the boots that had once been Richard's.

This straggling assortment of Medleys and near-Medleys and respected servants came at last to the boundary pinnold, which was no more than eight paces long and five wide; making a very small step across to the open forest.

Medley halted his followers. If the other side expected him to speak directly to them, they were mistaken. He preferred to send a herald.

'Richard,' he said, 'go ask them to send a man to speak clear in this business. Say we done the good thing – that we scoured and slaughtered as they wanted. April came now and all-us from Ghylls Hatch stay hale and healthy this long time. Say I know their worry and do understand much – but now *they* shall understand. Tell 'em we're passing to Mantlemass.'

The embassy filled Richard with pride. It was a little as if banners flew and trumpets sounded as he went ahead of the rest and stood halfway on the bridge to shout out his message. Only he was well aware of hesitation in the army at his back, of a kind of shyness – and looking at the opposing faction, all empty-handed, weaponless, strangely unferocious, he saw other Penfolds, different Ades, with Goodales, Grovers, Urrys, also a Crutten or two, and the Godsmark brothers who were young Tom's uncles.

Ahead of this crowd stood Old Grover, who was furnaceman at the iron mill well to the south-west of Mantlemass. He was a big, dignified man, a good leader.

Richard spoke out as his father had told him, then came to an end somewhat lamely. 'So now we done all,' he said, 'and shall go to Mantlemass, to bide wi' Dame Cecily and my uncle, Master Simon Mallory – seeing we're all but out o' victuals b'now.'

The moment the words were out he was scarlet with mortification. What better weapon to hand an enemy than the information that the garrison was starving?

'Sir,' said Grover, in the smoke-roughened voice of his trade, yet somehow gently and without any triumph, 'there's naun here but respect for Mus' Medley o' Ghylls Hatch. There's none'd wilfully harm him'n his, see you.'

'You threaten us!' Richard cried.

'Niver, niver that! But it comes years gone from Dame Cecily, naun other – diseases that pass one to one must be quenched out b'burning. And when your own grandfather took sick of the plague, she let naun of his rest till it were ashes. And the bed he breathed last on, rest him, that, too, she did burn – though it were her marriage bed.'

Richard was now as pale as he had been red. He mumbled, 'I'll tell my father . . .'

'He know – he know, wi'out more telling!' Grover cried. 'The little maid died under Ghylls Hatch roof. Evil now hang in that place. And how'd it come? Why – through a sorcerer's craft – any know that! Two evils in one, and twice the fire needed to rid 'em. Go back to Mus' Medley, then, and tell'm what he know well a'ready.'

There would be little need to repeat Grover's words, however, for his voice had risen till it resounded all about. As Richard turned to recross the pinnold, he saw his father grab at Harry's arm, and Harry shove it off so violently that Medley staggered, Harry came pounding past Richard and hurled himself at Grover, shouting.

'Stand back, now! Stand back and let us through! Weeks and months I kept from my wife and sons – for you and yours as much as any living – because my father willed it so. Let me by, then. I'll go to them now if I kill you doing it! Let me by, you sworly beggar!'

He hardly moved Grover, who took him by the wrists and held him.

'There's no malice in it, sir. Only what mun' be done. Last plague I lost my two sons that were away to Lunnon. I know your trouble, then. How you feel now, I did feel then.'

And as if ashamed for Harry's helplessness in this enormous grip, he let him go, and stepped back a little.

By then, Medley and Piers were plucking Harry away.

'His grief . . .' Medley said.

'Aye, sir.'

'We do all despair a little, Grover. Tired as dogs. Harsh work and cruel and much misery . . . But I'm not like to plead wi' you. You know that.'

'I know it, master.'

'And you know, too, that all I said should be – living close on our own ground – separated ... It did stop the sickness where it begun.'

'I know it, master,' Grover said. 'All among us know your wisdom.'

'But when I say – All's done – you do not trust me.'

'Any in the forest that know you trust you. They trust you to do best for all-us.'

'Yet you stay close lest I refuse to burn down my own house and hearth!'

'Ah, master,' said Grover gently. 'We need know you trust yourself.'

For a moment Medley stared at him almost in admiration, for such a compound of sense and stupidity would have been hard to match. He laughed. It was perhaps a slightly soured laughter, but the sound came.

'So be it,' he said.

'So we go crawling back,' Harry had shouted, 'beaten on our own ground by a rabble out of the forest!'

'Be silent,' Medley said. 'There's much to be done.'

They would heap brushwood in all the rooms, along the walls, in the centre of the floor. They had used pitch in destroying the stables, and there were two barrels left. The decision having been made, there was no further question from any one of them save Harry, but his sullen challenge had to go unheard. At first he held apart, refusing to take his turn in what went forward. But sheer frustrated energy had to be used up, and he began to toil with the rest. The men had been deployed to cut wood and carry it, as so often they had done for comfortable domestic purposes – to feed the hearth, to heat the ovens. Now they needed so much, much more. Then, one by one, in twos and fours and more, those who had been the besiegers, the strange enemy, took turn with the rest. From one side and the other they began to work together, falling back into old relationships that siege and separation had merely interrupted. The men had much to talk of, though they did it in low tones out of respect for the master and his sons. A quiet rejoicing began that after such ordeals they were still alive. Between them, by these great efforts, they would end an enchantment, they would dispel the last breath of the sorcerer's spell that had made the dreaded disease ten times more fatal than when it had been visited so many years ago on Ghylls Hatch. That earlier stroke had been from God, for some divine purpose that was humbly accepted but could not be understood. But this last, by every sign they knew, by every wickedness so easily recognized, had been the work of the Devil. He had struck at Master Medley through the unchecked arrogance of his eldest son, whose punishment had been the hardest … The reasoning was plain, acceptable, unchallenged.

They worked at their preparations over two long days. By the very nature of the business, everything must go. All that Medley would take away with him of his own was a small iron-bound chest that contained the few remnants of his origins. Whatever else happened he would fight, he would almost kill, to keep that. He wore the gold chain that Lewis Mallory had bequeathed him safe under his shirt. There was money to be brought out of the vault, too, for they had sold well at the end of last summer and they would need all they could find. But there would be nothing more. Nothing …

'Except only the books,' Harry had said, looking anxiously at Piers. 'The stud books, sir. The accounts and ledgers. To start all over again with never a written word to help ... There's little sense in that ... Piers? Piers, speak up – this is for you.'

'He said it should be all – then all it must be. Let it all burn – all. The place is cursed – let it burn and every stick and paper in it.'

Piers said no more. He looked sick, almost faint, but he did not speak again.

They were now all of them calm, knowing an end to be near, leaning towards it almost with longing, that it be done and over and past prayer. For Harry Medley most of all this day was full of both hope and torment. Now he longed to see the place down, its walls beaten to the ground, its ashes scattered. With it would go the tyranny he had made of it, the tragedy he had brought upon them all. In the last hour of the living house, his father ordered him to go through every room and closet to see that the preparations were complete. Piers and Richard had been sent elsewhere – to the kitchens, to the roof-thatch. Harry had the doomed place to himself.

He entered by the hall, where trains of pitch had been laid among the rushes, and then he was moving instinctively towards that small chamber where all the work of the place had been recorded and accounted. Here was the seed and the growing of Ghylls Hatch, the centre of life for his brother Piers. Almost against his will, impelled by an intense emotion near to hatred, Harry began dragging out the books, bound round in leather, enormous, laboriously written in many hands over the long years – opening one he saw a date that was somewhere about the time of his grandfather's birth. here were lists of purchasers, noble family names – Sackville, Sidney, Dallingridge, others less known. He turned the heavy pages, and the names of horses then darted out at him, many repeated several times – Ebony

V, Psyche II, Psyche III, and so on down to those he himself had known and ridden; others, like Violante, like Hera, long forgotten; dam such and such, sire so and so, sold to whoever, whenever ... They had their own place in time, in history, more than many a mortal man ... And to these creatures, ever since he could remember, he, Harry Medley, had been bound in slavery.

He looked up sharply, for he thought he had heard voices and some movement outside; but as he stood, head bent to listen, the silence took over again and he knew he was alone. As he straightened and turned back, he saw the lantern that hung always by the door. Had it been lit today by habit, though it could not be needed? Was it lit in preparation, to be hurled among the brushwood? Or had Piers already planned a last minute rescue of the precious records, knowing his father so well that he could count on his sympathy if it were heroically done? So, then, it would be horses again, the bondage over again ... In his present state of battered, unreasoning mind and exhausted body, Harry experienced a revulsion so intense, so powerful and relentless, it was as if his brain seethed up to white heat and might almost blow itself apart – might gush out like molten metal.

He shoved the books from him in utter disgust. Not again. Never, never again. Now he would be quit of it all, and the rest must be quit with him. They would turn to other things for their livelihood. They all knew it in their hearts, though it might be long yet before the admission was made finally and irrevocably. They would turn to iron, as they should have done years ago. He, Harry Medley, would be a master of iron at last, and he would find his true place in the world as he saw it. He took down the lantern and stood it within the mound of scrub that had been set up in the room. Then he kicked its side and the horn splintered, so that the flame, in the sudden draught, leapt and licked, lengthening to explore beyond the confining body of the lantern.

Immediately, as if denying knowledge of what he had done and seen, Harry turned on his heel and left the room, running back into the hall. Here all was quiet. The narrow door to the solar stairs hung open. He went through it and up the stairs and began to walk methodically through the house that he had known since he was born. And suddenly it was full of sounds and visions that he must take quickly into the safe storage of his memory. He recalled his mother sitting under the window to catch the light on the work in her hands, stitching fine, yet with a kind of impatience, glad always to leap up and rush outside to ride over the forest with that delight which he had never known ... He remembered the day of her death, his father's awful despair, his uncle coming from the Priory, his grandmother running down the track from Mantlemass ... He thought of Anne, the day he had first seen her, the day he had brought her home; and he went into the chamber that had been given over to them, and stood by the bed where his children had been conceived and born. He tugged down the bed hangings and piled wood over them, and ripped off the coverlet and threw it with the rest, thinking of how they had lit a fire above Cecilia's grave, and how he had been comforted by that fire. He would be so comforted again, and he frowned over the thought, for it seemed near madness to find comfort in destruction, to love this agent that consumed, but that cleansed and purified and in the long run made all new ... How had men ever made a new life before they discovered fire to make away with the old?

He moved on through the house, and now he was thinking of Piers, whose life had touched tragedy and never quite moved free of it. He thought of Catherine's mother, the strange wife that Piers had so early lost; and of how, returning to them at last, he had seemed even so to be parted from them by his troubles; and more at Mantlemass than at Ghylls Hatch, seeking comfort from his grandmother. Maybe for Piers, too, this holocaust would bring its blessing, forcing him to make himself anew.

For a second Harry was still, aware of what he was doing to Piers, knowing the books in the room below would soon, at the least, be smouldering ... Why had he felt himself fit to decide the matter? Why seen fit to add all this to the weight on his conscience?

It was now that he heard his father loudly calling, shouting to him to come out at once, for the business must be begun.

Harry went at once down the stairs and out into the April day, that was not bright, but palely sunny, the sky lightly misted.

'Piers and Richard are about it now, Harry. Take this torch and go to the upper room. Touch off what you can. I'll see to the matter here. Matt and two of the lads are gone to the roof. Bunce and Colin are through in the kitchens.'

He was calm but looked very worn. He might have appeared a man defeated, forced to an extreme and terrible step because he was too weak to fight for what was his own. It was not so. The rough wisdom offered him by Grover had saved him though it had destroyed his possessions. Because of it, he triumphed. He would never be doubted again. The forest, its people, its daily life, were his now until he died.

After they had touched off the wood and the pitch, the

men clustered outside and waited. They waited in total silence, their faces turned to the house, their eyes narrowed, their ears straining for what must come bursting forth. After the wet winter, even the thatch was slow. Then a wisp of smoke showed over the far gable, died, curled in a spiral of air, then suddenly changed into flame.

The house was nowhere near the proportions or endurance of Mantlemass. Ghylls Hatch had been little better than a scatter of buildings for many years, and only when Medley went there with his family after Roger Orlebar's death was there anything very substantial in the way of living quarters. Yet how it resisted destruction now. How firm the walls stood, how the rafters hauled at the crackling thatch and the thatch clung on, free of nesting birds that flew sharply and shrilly upward, of rats that darted from the smell and the sight of fire and leapt after safety. And indoors, how slowly the fires crept among oaken tables and chairs and chests, stools and beds and the softness of coverlet and cushion. Even the rushes on the floor, that burnt away in one quick flare when they were raked out of the hall, now held off an easy doom.

Medley looked at the sky.

'The sun's too hazy. If a downpour come to douse the work I doubt there'll be strength left in any of us to get to it again. Harry – inside and see how matters go. No, Piers – Richard! One's one too many.'

Harry ran inside. As he paused, uncertain where to look, there came from the farthest corners of the building a low, a steady roar. Smoke gushed into the hall, billowing up to the roof, tumbling to rise again, thickening and darkening, then fanning and thinning.

Ahead of him, in the little chamber where he had set the books burning, he saw that the fire was hardly begun.

The ancient leather, the thick parchment with its faded writing, defied destruction. His mind's wild eye filled suddenly with a memory of Piers's sick tragic face as he cried out *Let it burn – let it all burn – the place is cursed* ... Neither the cry nor the face, Harry saw now, had been that of a man speaking falsely, a man plotting to bring about his own self-centred purpose. Harry shivered in the heat and the smoke. His own madness, that same harsh, vain determination that had already destroyed so much for all of them, would destroy his brother's entire future.

He ran forward, knowing that he had done Piers a terrible injustice. He had indeed been willing to submit, he had been beaten to the ground and been ready to lie there despairing – but there was time even now to drag him to his feet instead of beating him still lower ...

Harry plunged into the room, the heat now making him gasp, intent only on making some restitution and leaving Piers at least a remnant on which to rebuild. Even if he died in the doing – he was bound to try. The smoke in the hall was thickening again, making him splutter helplessly as he began to drag at the great volumes, tall, broad, hideously heavy and unwieldy.

Then he heard Piers himself shouting, 'Harry! Harry, where are you? Come away! It's burning fast now!'

At the same instant, the smoke eddied, leaving a clearance and in it Harry, stooping over the books.

'You set them burning! You took great care, surelye! Let 'em die with the roof and the walls! It was to be a sacrifice – a sacrifice, not a slaughter! Never a slaughter!'

'It was you said they should go, you fool! Here – take these! Hurry!'

There was no time to argue, to explain, to say *After all I thought better of it ... I came to my senses ... I went to save them for you – for a legacy when I shall be gone* ... That was

nonsense, and he did not even know what he was thinking, the smoke so curdled his brain and blinded his eyes.

'Take what you can,' he said – or thought he said it, thrusting the books towards Piers, who looked as wild, as mad as Harry.

They began struggling together, gasping and coughing, spitting out the hot smoke, grabbing at the great weight of the books, tugging them, shoving them, stamping and slapping at the smouldering edges.

'The last,' Harry grunted. 'No more. Get out. Out ... The roof's coming in ... Get out ...'

Then he was calm again, hearing Piers yelling for help, knowing his father was with them, unprotesting, taking his part, breathing very hard and loud. Now indeed the fire had taken Ghylls Hatch to itself, and the heat and the din and the infernal smoke billowing and blowing, rising, falling, increasing one moment, diminishing the next and all the time growing hotter, ready to become flame, made a true hell of every moment. Harry hardly felt the skin shrivel along his fingers, but he knew his hair was singeing, his boots smouldering ...

Piers suddenly yelled out, 'Harry! Come back! Come back! Let it go! Come quickly!'

He seized Harry by the arm, and they both fell, sprawling over the floor among the smouldering rushes. Their father was dragging them up, grabbing at arms, sleeves, anything that gave a hold. Piers scrambled to his feet, but Harry was past it, he could neither breathe nor get any muscle to obey him. He lay heaving and retching and feeling the last breath going out of him, his lungs bursting, his heart right into his throat and ears ...

Then Richard was there, and Matt Ade, and the two of them heaved and dragged Harry outside. He gulped at the fresh April air, groaning and sick, Piers was bending over him, rubbing at his hair, slapping at his boot soles.

'Your hands, God help you!'

'No matter ...'

He struggled to his feet and thrust away from them all. He went staggering and stumbling down the far bank to where the water fell sharply over a ledge of rock. There was a pool almost the size of their own fishing pool below the fall, and he flung himself into it without any coherent idea of what he was doing, feeling as near death as a living man could. The bitter chill of the fast-flowing water was like steel blades on his skin, but the water salved and held him and brought his shocked brain back to him. He held up his raw hands and the pain made him groan. Now truly his falcon's feathers were altogether singed away and what remained was the plumage of a bird of fire.

He shook the water from his hair and eyes, dragged himself to his knees, then to his feet and struggled to the bank, his teeth chattering, his body shaking and twitching.

He saw Piers standing waiting for him, a great dark cloak held out. He dragged it round Harry's shoulders, begging him to come fast and strip off his wet clothes. There was fire enough, Piers said, half sobbing, to dry a drowning army.

'We'll get to Mantlemass, and Judith shall heal the burns ... Harry ... Harry ...!'

Harry began to plod on his way back to the others, his father already running towards him.

'Forgive me,' Piers said.

Forgive *me*, was what Harry should have answered. He said nothing.

High above, the smoke, now rising into the pale sky showed the work well doing. On the bank beyond, there was no smoke. The fires were out, the ashes stamped and scattered. The men had gone away. The siege was lifted.

12

At Mantlemass

Mantlemass was spacious, but the Mallorys had had it to themselves for many years and the addition of the Ghylls Hatch household could hardly go unnoticed. The room that Susannah shared with her sisters seemed now to Margaret and Elizabeth, who had had it to themselves lately, to be just right for two. Now back came Susannah, and bringing Catherine with her, since the child had attached herself to her cousin. With Medley and Judith, Harry and Anne and their two boys, with the attendant nurses and those personal servants who must not be dismissed for very charity and sweet reason, with Piers and Richard as well – there were bound to be times when the Mallorys felt hard pressed. Yet seen at table they made a handsome company – whoever might regret the invasion, Dame Cecily rejoiced. For her it seemed a return to the past, when she and her husband, Lewis, had seen their son and his wife, their daughter and her husband, at table each day. Dame Cecily was no fool, however, and it was hard for her as for any of them to see what would come next. It was for the son's family to look to Mantlemass for a home – when Simon's daughters married they would be entitled to table with their parents, at least for a while. Of her granddaughters, Dame Cecily loved Susannah and was as irked by Margaret and Elizabeth as she was by their mother. Of her grandsons, Piers was her dearest, with Richard not far behind; Harry she had never understood – there was an alien strain in him that had come through his father's father and grandfather. For Medley himself Dame Cecily had a feeling like no other she could name – respecting him because he had won her daughter and made himself a life almost from nothing; and sometimes considering him with a deep glance that was almost more than respect. Of all the big company at table, only Dame Cecily and Medley himself knew the strange facts of his birth. He had put them from him; she could not.

It was a month and more before Medley and his sons began to stir from the deep exhausted melancholy into which the events of the past months had beaten them. Then it was mid-May and the sun shone. It shone bright enough to cast a shadow behind which the past, though it could not be forgotten, could yet be concealed. So they stretched themselves a little; Harry's burnt hands grew a new pink skin; Anne took comfort from the children she still had and looked to others unborn; and Piers stacked away the Ghylls Hatch accounts, the scorched and battered stud books that he owed to Harry and for which, by pride or perversity, he could not be thankful; rather they seemed at this time a millstone, dragging him down. Of them all, Piers was the most beaten, the least ready to recover. Since that rebuff by the water's edge he had not been able to speak to Harry, and Harry would not be the first to bend. Richard was again in the situation of watching each in turn, uncertain which way either would jump. Richard's loyalty was all for Piers, but he knew that Harry would not long stay passive, and that there was still more striving ahead. When the future was finally spoken of among them, it would be Harry, for certain, who got in the first word.

Harry, indeed, spoke out just short of Whitsun, saying he thought fit to ride with Anne to Easingwell, for she was concerned to know the fate of her old home, and hoped for some word of her godmother, Dame Alison.

'Judith has said she'll care for our boys,' Harry told his father. The disasters and griefs she had endured had dried Anne's milk, and the baby was at nurse with Colin Crutten's young wife, Sukey, whose own first child had been stillborn. 'It will do Anne good to ride with me,' Harry said; then paused, looking awkwardly at his grandmother. 'I have forgotten, madam, that we must beg horses.'

'Speak with Henty. I know which you are like to choose, Harry Medley – that great-boned Ajax! But let Anne take my gentle Emerald.'

So in soft weather, Harry and Anne rode into Kent, with Colin for groom, and taking all gently came towards Easingwell in the afternoon of the second day.

They had stayed overnight where Harry and the rest had stayed years ago on the eve of his marriage – at the manor house of Mary Mallory's brother. Though the hospitality had been ungrudging, both had felt they were not altogether welcome. The talk was always turned away from inquiries about Easingwell, and when they left none came to set them on their way.

'They are wary on my father's account,' Anne said. 'He seem a traitor to them, no doubt. They think best they keep from knowing his kin.' She looked flushed and shamefaced. 'To think such matters ever come to smirch Sir John – so good and upright.'

'Think nothing of it,' Harry advised her. 'Another day

he'll home in triumph and they'll be all for him then. Such weathercocks are of little account.'

As they moved towards Easingwell there was some coming and going on the road, and when the trees opened to give a view of the place across the meadows, they saw that a flag flew above the tower.

'What if he returned in safety!' Anne cried. 'Say it should be my father, Harry – all forgiven and pardoned!'

His sight was longer than hers. The flag flew out well in the breeze, and the arms it carried, he saw quite clearly, were not those of Furnival.

'There are strangers there,' he said, reining in. 'The King may well have granted the manor elsewhere.' He looked anxiously at her stricken face. 'We should'a thought it could be confiscate, ' he said.

He feared Anne might break into tears at this, but he had overlooked the change in her. Anne had shed tears enough for a lifetime, and shed them alone; she would never again weep easily.

'Ride on,' was all she said.

When they came to the place itself they saw at once many changes. The drawbridge was gone, a high causeway led instead to the great doorway, though the portcullis hung still in its place. Harry left Anne with Colin and rode alone to the gatehouse. He inquired there, as any traveller might, the name of the lord of Easingwell.

'Sir Thomas Harking, sir,' the guard answered.

'Has he dwelt long in these parts?'

'Not so long.'

At this Harry offered a coin, and the man grinned and added, 'Nor he bore no arms till last Wednesday at earliest! The King knighted his money-bags! The place was Sir John Furnival's, but he got sent off for a traitor. Dwells in France, and safely, I pray God. If so be you should seek him there, say Timothy still keeps the gate.'

Harry nodded, wondering what to do next. He thanked the man and tossed him another coin, which he caught neatly.

'Dame Alison's all that's left of the old sort, master. Come you should seek her – she live in the Dower house across the park.'

Dame Alison was living with one servant as old, though not as deaf, as she was. The house smelt damp and dirty; more than the cellars would be rat-ridden, for sure.

'Oh God bless you, dear soul!' cried Anne, as her godmother fell weeping into her arms and clung to her trembling – a sad shadow of her old stamping lively self, gown torn, ruffles dirty, coif all askew on hair that was now as wispy as it was white. 'What come to you, in the name of Heaven, lady? Why are you here? Where's Marian, that tended you so long? And Rose? And page Dominic?'

'They went away – but Prue never left me. Prue's with me yet, as old as I am . . .'

'How do you two live?' cried Anne, her gaze shrinking from the shabby, squalid room.

'Ah, my dearest child, my lovely Anne – I had a fortune from my husband, well you know. I was bound to aid your father when he fled abroad, God help him . . . But what he left unpaid, near kin should pay – so they said. And little left at the end of it all but a noble – and that was Prue's.'

Then, as though she had so much bottled up in her it must gush out or the vessel itself would burst, she began a long recital of misfortune: how Sir John had sent word ahead that he was released but must go for safety into France; how he had asked her to get money from his bailiff and have it ready when he called on her ... All that went as planned, though she sent him away with more than was his. She said goodbye to him, blessed Master Medley who had helped him, and stood until the horses had clattered out of earshot; which, for her, was not long. She had had no expectation of what followed – of Easingwell being handed over to a new owner, with freshly minted arms and a bright new knighthood.

'Yet he was gentlemanly to me, saying I should have this house to end my days. And how, oh how I have prayed to God and his dear Mother to end those days, and take me from here, and give me peace – and Prue likewise.'

'You shall come home with me, godmother – you shall come to Mantlemass!' cried Anne, ignoring Harry's alarmed and scowling face.

'Nay, nay – I'll not leave Prue. Prue never left me, I'll never leave Prue. We see it out together, like some old year.'

Harry was muttering now, 'We cannot – we cannot take the servant, also. One is too many ...'

'Send to my uncle, then, madam. He is cousin more or less to all of us. Send to him – there's messengers enough in the land ... See he knows your plight!'

'Maybe, maybe ... But best I stay till I go, as 'tis said.'

Harry gave the servant money to buy food, and at last they sat down to supper with Dame Alison. They spent an uneasy night under damp covers in a creaking bed, and once Anne shrieked out that a mouse had run across her face. It was a relief when morning came and they could turn for home.

'I had sooner Easingwell were burnt to the ground like Ghylls Hatch,' Anne said bitterly, 'than see it now. I shall never know this place again, nor my father can never

return to it. Though the King grant him a full pardon, the fortune's gone that kept Easingwell – and he's too old now to find himself another.'

'But you shall have another,' Harry promised her. 'You know well we cannot stay for ever at Mantlemass, with my uncle's wife weighing the flour and counting the beans. There shall be another home – a better – and you shall have the jewels I swore to give you ... You do not believe me.'

She smiled a little, but she was nowhere near him in thought, worrying still over the old lady, puzzling how she might be helped. 'We must send to my uncle, Harry – though my father got nothing from him, he might be more willing to help a woman so old and wretched.'

'Your uncle's a man of much property, I recall. Sir John, told me long ago – his brother has many broad acres.' Harry paused, and then said, 'He is master of an iron mill – am I right?'

'I forget,' Anne said. This time her smile seemed a little warmer. 'It was as we came back from my uncle's country that we stopped at Staglye for mass.'

'You bewitched me, even then,' he said.

They were walking their horses on the heights north and west of Easingwell, and ahead of them the spread of the forest was already seen. Here, where they passed, it had been beaten back, defeated and tamed by axe and plough, and the farmsteads held their pleasant pastures in contentment. Maybe those who dwelt in these calmer places were complacent of their own advantage, and looked down on any who still dwelt in wilder spots – but to Harry these parts seemed exposed and dangerous. He held out his hand for Anne's and for a time they continued, slow in the sunshine, riding stirrup by stirrup.

He thought of her uncle's place, letting it back into his

mind from some corner where it had lain waiting all these years. When he went by Blackman's, by Plashets, when he heard of forest men shifting away to find quicker fortunes, he had always known this must be thought of some day. And when he spoke, as he had spoken both to Anne and to Richard, of some other place, some far place – though he might not have had strength or courage to name it, he knew today what place he had meant. It was that far forest called Dean, south-west many, many miles, lying in an alien part of England, beyond a broad river, almost into Wales.

It was a week at most after their return from Easingwell that word came from Dame Alison. It was brought by a fellow whose trade was in such errands, who plied through east to west, from Canterbury to Winchester, where some other of his kind took on the burden, pushing well beyond Gloucester and across the wild marches to the See of St David's.

'We've no use in sending to my uncle,' Anne said, when she had read the letter. 'News come almost as we left Dame Alison – sent to Sir John, not knowing he was gone. His brother died at the New Year. God rest him, then. So I have no father and no uncle.'

Harry took the letter and frowned over it; more than she had done, for he was a poor scholar. Dame Alison wrote of '*our poor cozin, Ellen*,' the widow, in sad straits with an ailing daughter, no man about the place, her son having long ago gone to London and never returned, so he might even be overseas. '*And how if he niver come again?*'

'Dear Heaven,' Anne said. 'The woes of women!'

'How if we ride that way?' said Harry, watching her.

'Harry! it is far – very far!'

'You rode it there and back as a child. I see no harm

come to you because of it.'

'What should we do for her? We never had so little of ourselves. Your father must speak soon what's to be done, surelye. We may not lick our wounds to eternity. Soon enough, Dame Cecily must find us tedious guests.'

'Yes, yes – it shall be spoken of soon,' he said. 'It must in decency be so.'

He wondered how he might broach the matter himself. For quite suddenly it had become of the first importance to know where he stood.

At supper a day later, Harry heard his father saying to Dame Cecily that he could no longer impose on her in the matter of horses, but must find himself his own.

'And also a means to living, madam. We may not for ever enjoy your good and loving hospitality.'

'Later,' she said. 'Let you rest, all of you. I have much comfort in your being here.'

'We shall build other quarters,' Medley said. 'There's ground of ours at Plashets. A good clearance, too. We might soon have pasture enough. It will be a slow start.'

They were at table at the end of the day. Save for Dame Cecily, the women had retired to other matters. As soon as Medley spoke the word *Plashets,* both Piers and Richard looked at Harry.

As they turned to him, Harry knew that his brothers were offering him what they believed he needed. It was a gesture of peace from Piers, of support from Richard, in whose gaze there was a great clarity and purpose. Harry knew that what he would say now would be false, yet he had to say it. He had not the courage to declare straight out and loud *I no longer care for Plashets; when I go, I go elsewhere* ... He must come to it by a different course – persuade his father what Plashets could hold for them, then leave it all for Richard. He should have thought towards this moment, had his forces mustered. But now there was no time, and the falsity must come first.

Medley looked towards him, paused a second, then turned to Piers. 'What would you say to Plashets?'

'The ground lie too low,' said Piers shortly.

'The best about Plashets is iron, sir,' Harry spoke almost before he knew he would, like a man leaping from a great height. 'You know well we spoke about this before – often enough. And once you did think more'n half kindly. Richard'll speak for me – he's a son you might lean on in this matter.'

'Lean?' said Medley. 'I'm not fit for leaning yet, I bluv!'

'The time, sir,' Harry said, 'the time come now. With Scotland beat, where shall the King turn – why against France! Guns, father. Every army need guns. There's iron enough in the Weald to arm a thousand galleys and forge five thousand cannon for the field.'

'So – never a tree upstanding,' Piers said, 'but all charked and consumed. How'll I build my stables, brother, when you got your cannon safely cast?'

'Iron at Plashets,' Harry said, 'means no stables needed more than a working row. You've to put yours up elsewhere.'

'Come back, Piers,' Medley said, but too gently.

Piers had gone, thrusting back noisily from the table, slamming out of the hall. Through the door open to the pleasant evening, they saw him go striding off across the court. Halfway, he paused and shouted back over his shoulder, 'Richard!'

Richard looked at his father, out through the door to Piers, and then at Harry. His father's face was expressionless, giving him no instruction, but Harry returned him a dark, challenging stare. Richard stayed. He knew his grandmother was watching him, that she wanted him to follow Piers, but he could not.

'Father?' said Harry.

'Truly I shall consider, Harry. You are right enough – I did think once ... For the time – let it rest a little. We are still weary ...'

'No! No, sir! Let it be spoke now – thought on now – decided now! How much longer are we to stay doddling and dozing and bewailing?'

Dame Cecily rose, saying they must make what plans they chose – so they were bound to rise with her, and maybe she thought she had broken the taut moment and the pressure would ease. But the moment she was gone from the hall, Harry was slapping at the table in his determination to be heard.

'Father, listen – listen, sir! If ever a finger pointed – if ever God gave a sign ... Our work destroyed – no means to make it over again till we gain new ground –'

His father broke in. 'Ghylls Hatch is still mine. The land is mine.'

'You never would build there again?'

'Not yet – no, not yet. But the land'll recover – the weather shall heal it. There's plenty stone for the digging to build afresh ...'

Harry changed his ground, reworded his challenge. 'When, then? When?'

'Two years should cleanse it.'

'Meanwhile we live – how?'

'As foresters live. How else?'

'No!' Harry said.

He spoke very loudly and no one answered. The word travelled the hall and returned, hanging about them with terrible and unabating force, echoing on and through their minds – Medley's, Richard's; Harry's, who had flung down the challenge and was now shaking, not with anger as so often before, but with the intensity of his purpose. Here and now and finally his future must be determined, as a man in his own right, not even as the eldest son, not even as his father's child, his mother's dearest – but as Harry Medley, as himself, with his own family, his own stake in the future, his own hostages.

He heard his father sigh. It was such an old matter, this clash of wills, yet today there was a difference. Because of time and events, the one who had been stronger had lost much of his power.

'Well, well,' Master Medley said, 'if we must speak of Plashets – then one day soon – we shall speak of Plashets . . .'

His weary tone at once dismissed and acquitted Harry. What he had thought best he saw was second best. The die was cast, then.

'I said it should be now, father. So I must decide what you're too weary to decide.' He waited for Medley to speak, but he was silent. 'As soon as may be, sir, I shall be gone from here, and my wife and sons with me.'

Medley rose, then, straightening his shoulders with difficulty, crossing the hall as Piers had done, but with a heavier tread. And as Piers had done, a pace or two, outside, the evening light now deepening, he paused and looked back, and called, 'Richard?'

Richard hesitated. He looked at Harry and his challenge but could not take it up.

'I did ever say – not if you went after some other country, brother.'

'Aye, so you did,' said Harry. 'So be it, then.'

Richard rose, and went after his father, pausing long enough on his way to touch Harry's arm.

But Harry shook him off.

13

Parting

A feeling of change stirred throughout all Mantlemass by nightfall of that same day. And in every chamber where one or another prepared for rest, and further, among the servants, even, the matter was spoken of. Because of it, life at Mantlemass seemed to hesitate.

Unlacing his jerkin, Medley said to Judith, 'We have lost Harry.'

'It had to come.'

'*Had* it so?' He frowned, for if he had ever thought it might come to this he had quickly laughed off the thought.

'I see it long since, husband – as so should you.'

'Hard to lose an eldest son . . .'

'And yet, my good love,' said Judith, in her plain foresty voice, 'you and that eldest son did never quite settle, each to each. What could come of it, then, but this?'

'My own father's in him, Judith – that pride and that strength never come to me. Only there's a difference. My father had a nobility about him; but Harry's hard and harsh as the iron he dreams of . . . And then my grandfather – my father's father, not old Tom Bostel, rest him; he must have had great pride – strong pride and power – some say cruelty. There's that in Harry, too.'

'I never heard you speak before of your grandfather.'

'I never saw him. My own father saw him naun but the once . . . I did plan to speak of him fully before I die – and that would've bin to Harry!'

'There's time. He's with us yet.'

'Aye, but this is to tell the eldest son, and since the eldest son choose to go away about his own business, then the second must be heir, surelye. Piers shall be eldest son, once Harry go – and any telling shall be to him.'

Judith smiled a little, knowing what he would never quite learn of himself – that his struggles with Harry were founded in an old jealousy, the boy's mother having been so wrapped up in him; that Piers he loved best because he was most like her; and that Richard, who had killed her, had had to wait for his father's affection until the misery was past. Harry was the one who had resisted Judith, yet without the indirect necessity posed by Harry's marriage, she thought secretly that Medley might never have paused to consider the matter of making her his wife.

'And I do doubt Richard a little,' she heard him say out of the muffling of his shirt as he dragged it over his head.

'Richard?' She could not believe that, and not only because he was as close to her as her own child would have been. So long as Susannah stayed at Mantlemass, Richard would never go elsewhere.

'He speak often enough of digging and smelting and such matters. And I see that maybe it must come to us. Iron's moving in where wood was master. It's not only cannons that must be in the making, Judith – I found that out when I went to London for Sir John. The King'd go overseas, so they said, wi' cooking ovens carried on carts – and the cooks working even on the march.'

'Aye, then, maybe it should be thought on.'

'It is *thought* on,' he said testily. 'But I thought too long, I reckon. Now Harry's far past Plashets in *his* thinking – he needs be all his own master. It's clear in his eye. These last months did harden him greatly. Sometimes I fear for Anne ...'

Judith shook her head. 'No need. There's one softness in Harry and all of it for Anne. More, even, since the child died ... Now be generous wi' Harry,' she urged him. 'Let him go, since he must, but let it be in kindness. Otherly, later on you shall be for ever reproaching yourself – and I will not love you sad.'

He scowled and snorted. 'You think me so great a fool?'

'Aye,' said Judith fondly. She thought how, when she was a girl of fifteen, and gone to keep house for his mother's father, old Tom Bostel, Medley had come one day to his grandfather's cottage, and she had been pulling the washing off the line. That was the day she knew certainly he would get his master's daughter for his wife; she had said goodbye to her own hopes that day ... She thought of the despairing girl she had been and smiled at the ways contentment could come – hers had found her through tragedy.

'A fool! A great fool – an *old* fool!' Medley was saying, but his irritation was easing into a better humour. 'Tell me some kinder name you might call me – then I'll sleep easy.'

'Let your conscience, not your vanity, send you a fair night,' said Judith, austerely smiling. 'And let tomorrow bring a better day.'

In their own chamber, that was on the far side of the wide gallery and had windows facing down towards Staglye – and you could hear the bells rung there when the weather was right – Harry had said to Anne, 'We shall go to your uncle's place. I told you this could well come about – but your uncle's death has spurred me on. And what your godmother tell of Dame Ellen's situation.'

She answered, 'Yes. Yes, one day we'd best go.' She frowned slightly, and her voice rose as she understood what he was telling her. 'But not yet, Harry? Why should we go yet?'

'Your uncle's widow may think fit to move away. You told me once that her married daughter lives nigh Gloucester. She may well go to her. Such places as your uncle's tumble fast – decay sets in as the last door closes. And there'd be a-plenty greedy hands stretched out to grab the iron working.'

'We must not go yet, Harry! I recall it as a long hard journey. The baby's still so small. What if he fall sick? Or if Jack take a fever?'

'You and your father made all but a winter journey. It is summer now.'

'How long, then? How long shall it take us? With the children – with a servant or two and what we have left to us of belongings? And with a pack animal – or at best a cart. That's no fine galloping order! We must go very slow, surelye. We are all but into June. How shall we rest until winter? And the weather may stay us. The roads are not as they were – any know that. And the monasteries all pulled down or abandoned, Harry – then where shall we find shelter? The fine priory guest houses are all gone – and the abbeys ...'

Her voice trailed away wretchedly. She was afraid to look at him, dreading a furious face. But he had never been anything but gentle with her, or needed to be other He laughed at her fears, but softly, taking her by the shoulders, teasing her, kissing her cheek.

'Anne, dear soul – be easy. I shall care for you as

though you were some holy relic.'

'What assurance is that?' she cried. 'Holy relics are not to be spoke of nor thought on – so says our lord the King. And they call him Harry, too!'

'You must trust me. I know what come best ... And I know few husbands'd take time to wheedle and coax, but rather make fists, and slam 'em down, and roar out *This shall be*! Yet it shall be, Anne. It shall be.'

'I must leave all I know, then? Your father – my only father, now. And dear Judith. And Dame Cecily and your brothers; and Susannah and the rest ...'

'I shall be with you and watch over you. We shall be making a life that is truly our own life. And I shall be my own master at last – not only my father's steward caring for dumb beasts too tame to answer when I shout.'

Anne was unsmiling. 'So it is that. You must be master.'

'Anne – I am all but thirty year in age. It must be soon, then.'

'Must! Must!'

'Aye, must! You said once *Whither thou goest* ...'

'You were master in your father's absence,' she said.

Her tone had changed, had taken on a note that deeply troubled him. He feared what was coming and strove to fend it off. She would speak what he had hoped need never be spoken now. He had convinced himself that the time had come and gone and she had chosen to stay silent. But now he knew he had cheated himself, that it was all the time between them, and that silence itself was separating them ... He put up his hand, almost as if he would cover her mouth ...

'See to it, sir,' she said, in a clear but distant voice, 'that you do not master another of our children to his grave.'

'Oh Anne,' he said. 'Anne, Anne ...' He sank down on the chest at the bed-foot, and sat there with his hands on his knees, his eyes closed, a terrible naked grief in his face. Anne did not comfort him, but moved away, turning her back, standing near the window to brush her hair and braid it. 'I did think you had forgiven everything – forgiven me everything,' he said.

'*My* father had to be saved – *my* begging sent Master Medley away to seek help for him. Had he never gone from home – then it could not have happened as it did. But it would have happened, one way, t'other way, if it were the will of God. I can accept God's will, as any must. Only see you make no new disaster grow out of your own human vanity.'

He remembered his father saying: *When the King speak out . . . in council . . . at table*, and so on. He remembered the stone tossed *sharp into the great pool of all England* . . . So it had been for them when Sir John was imprisoned. So, if he faced the truth, it was now for him. For the King planning war, fortune was thus flung at the feet of the armourers, of whom Harry knew he would be one . . . How puny a boast, then, that he should be *master.*

There was silence between husband and wife. Anne continued plaiting her hair; Harry sat still and purposeless.

At last he said, rousing himself and moving his shoulders as if to free them of some weight, 'Then stay. Stay here at Mantlemass until all's ready. Then I'll send. I shall go alone, I now see – and send later for you and the boys.'

'What if it be winter before you send?'

'Then you must not set out until the spring.'

'A year, maybe, then, and we shall not meet.'

'So it seem.'

Anne had done all she must to her hair, but she took long about setting the brushes by, and then poured water from the ewer and washed her hands, and dried them slowly. As slowly and with a careful modesty she laid her chamber robe by and took her place in bed. She was fatigued by what she had forced herself to say, but thc words had already been left too long, they had festered a little. She was very far now from the excitable, carefree girl who had become Harry's wife, but she felt the promise of a kinder future, though it might be distant some way, when her heart would be lightened and there would be true loving between them once again.

'So I am to wait a year,' she said, knowing he must be rallied, but unable to change his mood by softness, as he would have wished. 'Then am I to travel all those weary miles with no better company than some lumpkin servant?'

Harry looked up and half smiled. 'Now Anne – Anne, that's a shade over-womanly and capricious, so I'd say. What else, then? What else must you do?'

'For Jesu's sweet sake, Harry, stop nabbling and come to bed . . . I must travel when you travel.'

Harry never declared his purpose, there was no need. He laid his first plans in the forenoon of the following day and within another hour or two the news was far beyond Mantlemass and spreading rapidly about the forest.

'Have you thought again? Will you come?' he asked Richard.

'No, Harry. But I am happy you would be willing to take me.'

'Speak to Susannah, then. Her eyes are half out of her head.'

'She should know better,' Richard said.

Only his grandmother made some attempt to dissuade Harry, calling him to her in her own parlour, where she was sitting with old Jess Truley, her companion of so many years, and letting him stand before her like a rebuked boy. Jess had risen in a flurry to leave them alone, but Dame Cecily had told her to sit down and stop fidgeting.

'Think more of your father, Harry.'

'I have thought.'

'Life shall never be the same for him after this. To go so far . . . You had as well be dead.'

'Forgive me if I think otherly! It is all determined, madam.'

'I know well what he suffers – I, too, lost a son. I lost him before his death, long before his death – as your father must lose you. By the grace of God I saw him often before he died – but he was the son of the Church, not mine any longer.'

'We shall meet again, grandmother. Anne has made the journey before – and shall do so again, no doubt of it.'

'I am getting to be an old woman, Harry.'

It was anguish to Harry to be so talked at in front of Jess Truley. 'Any son needs growing and be his own man,' he said, his voice roughening as it still did under stress. 'That's good sense enough. I reckon any'd be dunch to do different.'

'Many sons will be patient and wait for their inheritance. Though I do see since Ghylls Hatch went, there may seem little to inherit.'

'Let be,' said Harry, hating her and loving her. 'I am a new man a'ready – born out of all that misery. Niver to be the same agin. I know what I must do. I'll do it, then.'

'Aye well,' she sighed. 'God keep you. Pray for me.'

Harry left her, trying to sustain his anger – even envying her; for though he might be stubborn as any man born to that stubborn countryside, he had not her quality of pride, and might never learn it.

Downstairs in the hall, he found Colin Crutten waiting patiently to speak to him. He was a tall young man by now, modest rather than shy, loyal and devoted.

'Mus' Harry,' said Colin, 'it's being spoken that you'll be going out of these parts.'

'Well, then, it's spoken truly. So I shall.'

'And shall you take servants, sir, or find 'em as you may?'

'Are you set to come with me?'

'Sir – it do seem middling sensible,' Colin answered, 'that I should make one.'

'What's sensible in that?' asked Harry, more to disguise his pleasure in Colin's request, than to appear capricious or over-masterly.

'You forgot, then?' Colin half frowned, half smiled. 'It's my Sukey's the wet nurse. How shall she not go along? So both-us must go wi' you – that's the sense of it.'

'Of course!' cried Harry, who had indeed been so much wound up in his own affairs that he had clean overlooked the connection. 'Both – both on you! D'you think I'd part husband and wife?'

Colin was flushed with the success of his approach, though he had been taken aback to discover Master Harry did not know who was nursing his own son – his father, his brothers, could never have done so. But Colin was not one to mull and mumble over his doubts, and such thoughts were soon gone. He became a hot recruiting officer for his fellows.

'How many to go, sir? Shall you speak wi' my mother's sister's son – Dan Morphew – Youngest Dan, that is? Morphews have cousins in Dean, sir – went that way a two-three year past. They'd be skilled furnace men by now.'

On a high wave of excitement that men would follow him of their own choice, Harry went on his way, saying over his shoulder as he strode from the hall, 'Send'm to me, Colin.'

It was perhaps the best moment he had experienced in his life save for all matters to do with Anne.

There was much to be planned. It would take them time to prepare. No one opposed or hindered. The decision was made, Harry would not relent unless for some unforeseen disaster, so it only remained for the rest to help as best they might. Perhaps, Harry thought, a shade grimly, their chief purpose now was to see the back of him, for over and above horses there was a waggon provided, with a hooped hood for shelter, and a sturdy-built cart with solid wheels that was made by the Mantlemass joiner. It was deep-sided and fitted with raves that deepened it still more – making it very fit, the joiner claimed with pride, for the carrying of young children. Jack was of an age to scramble in any forbidden place, and Anne was concerned for the wisdom of fitting extra boards, imagining him climbing up and balancing, and slipping, and being thrown out on his head in the dust, and breaking it, and dying by the wayside. No one felt able to laugh Anne out of forebodings about her children ...

In the waggon they stowed bedding that was mostly of coarse sacking stuffed with straw; so much had been destroyed at Ghylls Hatch that they were bound to depend on what Mantlemass could give. Dame Cecily turned out all she could for them, and Mistress Mary found much that she could spare, pressing upon Anne as a parting gift, a pair of fine linen sheets, the hems all embroidered. Judith spent hours in the Mantlemass stillroom, regretting her own lost supplies, but managing much pickling and conserving. They were to take bags of meal, and hams that would last the journey if the weather was kind; honey and honey cakes baked very hard, spiced with ginger; also dried figs, dried apples in leathery rings threaded on sticks. Also salves and medicinal drinks, in bottles of earthenware protected and kept cool in thick jackets of plaited straw. They took lard and oil, goose grease, meats potted under butter that might or might not stand the journey. They took thread and needles, shears and two bolts of home-woven cloth. Then knives and cooking-pots – that would make them clatter, Anne said, like an army of tinkers on the road. They took grain, onion seed, many cuttings of herbs stuck into a pan of earth and sand; and most important, tools – spade, saw, mattock, axe, rake – with a supply of nails and iron rings; good hempen rope; tallow and rushlights and oil . . .

Then into the little rave-cart, the three girls put toys for the children – a wooden horse that ran on wheels, a stuffed rag ball, a rattle for the baby. Susannah would have liked Catherine to give Jack her favourite hobbyhorse, only she looked so tragic at the thought it seemed best forgotten. But she parted with a box of sweetmeats she did not altogether like.

At last there seemed nothing more that could be needed, and nothing more, certainly, that could be conveyed without another small cart. So they came almost suddenly to the last hours at Mantlemass, with all prepared for a journey which could only take them the better part of the summer. A new countryside ahead, strangers dwelling there; and maybe not the waiting roof they hoped to find . . . Only the farewells remained to be said.

14

Phoenix

They would leave in the second week of June; that would give them long days, warm nights and a moon that week to set them well on their way. Colin would drive the waggon, turn and turn about with Youngest Dan Morphew, and they would share the driving of the cart with Sukey. They would have four riding horses between them; Dame Cecily had given Emerald to Anne, and let Harry choose three more – this last she offered with a slightly grim expression. On Sunday all the household went down to worship at Staglye, and Father Oswald came back with them to Mantlemass. Nothing remained to be done – the supplies were stacked, the waggon and the cart needed only a horse between the shafts of each, clothes were in bundles, the air was full and heavy with expectation of the morrow. Nothing like this departure had ever troubled the daily life of Mantlemass.

The priest blessed all that would make the journey – the waggon, the cart, stores, horses, dogs; men, women and children. In the early evening he sang vespers with all the family; then went on his way. Harry walked with him to the Mantlemass boundary, then watched him down the track. It was the first farewell and it clove into him like the stroke of an axe, full of pain and portent. He walked slowly home, knowing that home was here no longer. The evening was very still, blackbirds whistling, the trees now in total leaf, their lovely skeletons clothed and modest.

When Harry reached Mantlemass, Colin was looking for him. Having attached himself to Harry he was jealous in attending him, intercepting messages that others were set to carry, and delivering them himself.

'Master Medley seek you, sir. He say to send you – to ask you to go to him indoors.'

Harry had been waiting for this summons. For one thing he needed money, had not asked for it, and trusted his father to deal fairly by him. Though they had lost Ghylls Hatch and could not be profiting, as they should, by a new season's trading, the last years had been good years; and since all three brothers had always had opportunities to pursue their own dealings, Harry was not penniless. But two other matters than money filled his mind as he sprang up the stairs to find his father – his own great desire that they should not part in coldness – and the secret. The secret of the strangeness of Medley's life, some peculiarity of his birth that had enabled him, the son of a servant at Mantlemass and a man who would not marry her, still to be accepted by Lewis Mallory as a suitor for his daughter. *I shall tell it to you one day*, Medley had said, *you being the eldest son* ... Harry's heart warmed to the father he was turning away from, who yet seemed ready to keep a promise made a long time ago.

He went into the room with a very open expression, finding his father sitting at the table he had used for writing since coming to Mantlemass. His chair was thrust back and he gave every appearance of patience – so that Harry found it necessary to apologize.

'Sir – I have kept you waiting.'

'I had best not complain,' Medley answered. 'You'll not do so again.'

His voice was level, he spoke carefully and courteously, his speech clear of foresty inflexions. He wore his good doublet, which in fact had belonged to Simon Mallory, and the gold chain that Simon's father had willed to him. He looked handsome, Harry thought, with his greying hair, his bearing of great confidence that was tinged with a gentler quality. That quality was sorrow, and when he recognized it Harry saw, with a sinking of the heart, that this encounter would be harder than he had hoped for.

'Well, then, Harry,' his father said, 'you are to do as you wish, be as you wish – you shall become your own master. Never suppose I do not understand your going. Only I wish with all my heart it might be otherwise.'

'Thank you, father.' Harry hesitated, shifting his weight a little. 'And I wish it need not be – I, too, wish that.'

'You wish it less than you wish for your own freedom?'

'Freedom to make my own mistakes . . .'

'I'd never plead with you – but if you thought again, it could be a fresh beginning for us all.'

'I have thought, and I have decided.'

'Then tell me all your plan once more,' Medley said, very even in his tone, as if they discussed some daily matter.

Harry went again, keeping his patience, over the road they would follow, short of any trouble, and the cities they would enter, and how, when they reached that other forest at long last, they would seek out Dame Ellen Furnival; and from there all was conjecture, but conjecture high with hope and confidence.

'It may go well, one way, t'other way,' his father said. 'In the matter of monies, Harry – I thought best to make a division of my fortune at this time – if fortune it may be called. As if I had already died, see you. You shall have your portion; Piers and Richard I trust must wait some time longer.' He looked up and smiled slightly, then shoved two leather money-bags across the table. 'Stow them safe now. I have been just in the division. Only I am giving you the portion of the second son – since Piers must take your place with me as eldest.'

Harry flushed, from his hair right down into the collar of his shirt. His father's totally unexpected attitude filled him with outrage.

'As I stand here now, sir – at this moment – who am I, if not your eldest son?'

'You will be gone tomorrow.'

'As you hand me my inheritance – you hand it to the eldest son.'

'Harry, you have chosen to be your own master rather than my son. I am not punishing you – I am dealing fairly with all three of my sons.' He looked deeply into Harry's furious face. 'Take up the money, Harry. If you think to shame me by refusing it, you cannot do so. I am dealing justly. Accept what is yours. I am in no mood to part in any anger.' With that he removed the gold chain from his neck, with its fine design of linking and its big medallion, saying, 'Let me give this into your hand. It was your grandfather's, as well you know. Let me see you wear it.'

Half bemused now, he was so taken off his guard by what was happening to him, Harry did take the gift and slip the chain over his head.

'When you wear it one day in your own fine hall, Harry, let it recall your Mallory blood. Also the Jolland blood, that comes to you from your grandmother. Remember all these things, and that you are entitled to the emblem – *the lark and the laurel.* I have not myself seen fit to use it, but you may use it on your liveries.'

'You see me growing very fine, sir.'

'Yes. I do see you so . . . The medallion is in two halves and opens. You will find the emblem engraved inside.'

As his father spoke, the distance between them was all the time lengthening, until they seemed to be facing one another across the table as cautious diplomats, as lawyers or politicians, or as sages whose talk is all of matters impersonal.

'What more can I say – save to wish you well?'

'Sir, you can tell me of yourself – as you promised to. You speak only of my mother's family. But tell me of *your* father, *your* grandfather . . . For how am I to make up my pedigree only from the distaff side?'

'How have I made up mine? I have chosen to live in the world with only one name, Harry. I have given you more. You should contrive, I think.'

'Tell me, none the less,' said Harry, his voice hardening. 'It is little to ask. Tell me, then.'

'No, I shall not tell you. If it go forward at all, then it shall go forward through Piers. I said that such matters are told to the eldest son, for his eldest son –'

'Piers has no son!'

'Piers is young enough to forget his sorrows and take another wife.'

'You are playing God with me, Master Medley – and with my brother, too. I do demand to know. It is my right. I do insist you tell me! I do *insist*!'

'No, Harry,' his father said, neither cold nor cruel, neither taunting nor triumphant, but flat and sure as daylight. 'Be certain I shall not.'

Harry heard his voice rising and tried to drag himself back from fury, but could not.

'Then – are we to part in anger?'

'I am not angry, boy.'

'But I am angry!' Harry roared out, his fury leaping from him like some tiger. 'By God, you treat me very ill! I cannot ever forget it! I am disinherited and I have not deserved such! I see what it is – I see now, indeed I do! You blame me for all that come about at Ghylls Hatch – and this is to be your revenge!'

For the first time, he scored a hit. The very baseness of the accusation made Medley jerk up his chin as if he had received a direct blow. The very baseness of it, such was Harry's state of mind, forced him on to more, to worse. His wretchedness poured out of him, and if he sounded full of hatred and vengeance, the hatred was equally for himself, the victim of his own hot-headed abuse. He plucked at the gold chain and tried to break it and fling it down, to reject it and with it everything he might claim to be. But the links held, and he merely looked and knew he looked, like some petulant, stamping child. He could almost have taken his father by the throat, as sons before this had done, even fatally – but at least that was avoided.

He was making a great noise, and it would be heard halfway round Mantlemass. It was not surprising that the door should open and Judith rush in, full of anguish at what was taking place. At least her coming broke what seemed like a dreadful spell, utterly entangling him.

He pushed past her rudely and flung out of the room. He went striding to the head of the stairs, calling at the top of his voice for Anne.

She was already looking up at him from the foot of the wide shallow stairway, her face white, her eyes enormous.

'Harry . . .? Oh do hush!'

'Call Sukey. Fetch the children. We'll not wait till morning. Now. We're going now. All's ready, no need for delay. We set out now, Anne – do you understand what I am saying?'

'I hear you. I cannot hope to understand!'

'Take off that mawkin face and get about the business! We're not resting one more night under this roof!' Then he roared for the servants. 'Colin! Morphew! Come here to me, damn you!'

The house stirred to Harry's bellowing, to the noise as he clattered down the stairway and across the hall. Now he was set on a course as sure as any planet, and he could not break free and turn back. Pride, disappointment, the terrible sorrow that came from parting in anger, drove him far past any good sense. He behaved like the madman his uncle Simon Mallory called him, who tried vainly to block his way at the foot of the stairs ...

Then the place, that had been resting in its evening quiet, came suddenly awake and full of people roused and anxious. Servants ran up and down with last items to add to the luggage already stowed. Sukey came down with the baby, her eyes round with surprise and fright – and Mary ran as if to prevent her, only Judith held her back.

Outside, by the waggon, Piers argued with Harry and Harry all but knocked him down for his trouble. Then Anne came out holding Jack by the hand, the boy sleepy-eyed and almost stumbling.

With Anne's coming, the scene shifted from the house, and everyone was jostling about the waggon, about the cart. Dame Cecily came out, hurrying and determined as if for sure she would put an end to the hubbub. But when she looked at Harry's face, contorted with his own furious misery, and at Anne, pale and speechless, she turned back ... Master Medley was coming out of the house, but she put her hand on his arm and stayed him.

'Let him go. There is nothing to be done ... Too late ...'

She stayed beside him a moment, resting her head

against his shoulder, and he put his arm round her, knowing she must need support. As indeed he did, too. He stood looking most of all at Anne, who seemed to be pushed about among them as if she hardly knew what was happening. *How am I to trust you with a wife?* he had asked Harry once. Or some such words. He wondered afresh, and as Dame Cecily went on indoors, he moved towards Anne – and as it happened she came running as if he had called her and threw herself into his arms.

'My dearest, my only father ... What come to make all this? He seem mad and there's naun I can say to stop him. But we'll not travel far before morning – and then he shall ride back to make his peace.'

'Let be,' he answered. 'I have greatly offended him and now I see he's no longer a man to offend. Many a father, I daresay, opens his eyes too late.' He kissed her and held her warmly. 'Go in peace, my dearest girl, and God help you make the best you may.'

Suddenly the hurly-burly was finished. The last knot was tested, the horses saddled and bridled, Sukey in the cart with the children, Colin taking up the reins, Dan Morphew climbing into the waggon, the spare horses tethered and waiting, the dogs rushing and barking.

'Anne!'

Anne turned away from Medley, paused to embrace Susannah, kissed Piers, Richard – then went to where her husband stood waiting for her at Emerald's stirrup.

'You have this chance,' she said to him in a low voice. 'For God's sake, speak to your father. You dare not part like this.'

'Mount,' he said, 'and we're away.'

'Harry, I beg you. Do this for me. I beg you.'

'Come now – I'm waiting to see you jossed up.'

'He will not come to you – how should he?'

'And how should I go to him?'

He swung her up, and the boy at the horse's head stepped back as she gathered up the reins.

Anne said once more. 'Go to him!' Then moved on because she could no longer endure to look at any one of them. She heard the horses stamping, and within seconds Harry had ridden up behind, leading the two spare mounts, had moved alongside, had passed her. The waggon creaked and rumbled on the summer-hard track; the cart, lighter, chattered as it followed. The baby cried once and was hushed by Sukey. Only Jack, wide awake now, leant over the tail of the cart and waved and called and called goodbye.

The long summer day was not quite ended. The sky still held a pearly light. The flush from the west was matched by the first upward glow of the moon. The blackbirds that had sung for Harry as he walked back from seeing the priest homeward were quieting now, but a thrush still sang, as if waiting for the first notes of the nightingales.

They rode on up the long familiar track that would show them the ashes of Ghylls Hatch before it carried them over the brow to westward, which would in its turn take from them the last sight of Mantlemass. Harry would not look back, Anne dared not. They rode in silence through the forest. As dark came down, reluctant, delicate, lifted on the moon's back, deer moved and owls swept the sky. They came by the ancient forest pale and moved among lighter woodland, little more than a fringe to pasture. In this manner they took what was still a familiar way until half the night was done, plodding somewhat in the bright moonlight that showed them soon a river with a ford.

'Rest here till morning,' Harry said.

He spoke very quietly, wearily. He lifted Anne down and they stood together.

'I never slept under the sky before,' she said.

He held her close to him, pressing his face against hers and shivering. Her cheeks were running with tears; but not her own.

On the first day, they headed south along the river. There was a good track that carried waggon and cart without too much difficulty, since horse-drawn barges took this way seaward. Soon, the downs rising against the clear sky at noon, they came to the pilgrims' path, an underhill track that, if all tales were true, could carry them eventually, changing character but not direction, even as far west as Gloucester – or, had they wanted to turn in their tracks, as far east as Canterbury. But at least in these first stretches that they came to, the way was very rough and they made slow progress. It was six or seven years since the monasteries had been dissolved by the King and their inmates scattered; so, too, with those shrines to which pilgrims had travelled regularly, almost throughout the year, if the winter were mild. The way had become neglected, its surface breakin~ and grassing-over with lack of use; cattle had been driven along it in rainy weather, making deep pits and ruts that froze or baked according to the season. Often brambles had grown forward from the verges, casting their thorny trailers ahead of them, as if to clasp in greeting those which stretched out from the farther side. At some points, the road had been ploughed by some greedy farmer adding to his acres and there, even in this dry weather, the going was hard.

In spite of fine weather, that was a difficult day. Anne was exhausted from the tumult of the previous evening and Harry so wound about with his own troubles that he barely spoke. The servants took their mood from the master, Jack grizzled, the baby was fretful. For as many as three days, indeed, this mood continued, though the weather stayed fine. The quiet here, the lack of traffic or any sign of life save sheep, added to the gloom. Though the downs reared, the countryside itself was very open, and they all felt unprotected. On the second night they slept again out of doors. On the third, Colin, having gone in search of eggs, returned with the news that the farmer would let them rest overnight in one of his barns.

Perhaps it was the sweet new hay smell that made them sleep sound and wake refreshed; or else, speaking for the first time to strangers and finding them kind, their burdens seemed lightened. Either way, it was on this fourth day that the mood changed. They set out that morning with fresh bread and milk in the waggon, the farmer and his family waving them on their way. Sukey began to sing softly as she drove the sturdy little cart in the wake of the great waggon.

'My father and I rid our horses along the tops of the downs, that time we come this way,' Anne said. 'And there, standing agin the sky – aye, truly, standing, though it sound dunch – was the great shining wall of the sea.'

'I see it from above the town, often,' Harry answered. He cleared his throat as if his voice, lacking exercise, had rusted.

'Take Jack, husband, and ride up the ridge. Let him see the ocean.'

'Later,' he said. 'When we bait.'

This was the first exchange they had had, save for necessary matters. So then Colin and Dan began talking together, and Sukey sang louder. Jack ran by the cart snatching at butterflies, and tripping, but finding a tumble no worse than funny. Even at such a pace, Harry thought, they should be at Chichester by nightfall or a little sooner.

That load that was on his mind and his heart, that spread about his whole body, so that he stooped, eased a little. He straightened himself and stretched, and next time Jack fell, his father swept him up and rode him shoulder high. And sure enough, that late afternoon, he took the boy on his saddle and rode with him to the high ridge and looked down and over and out to the sea. Westward, the downs declining to the plain where the river ran in, they saw the great church of St Richard.

Harry was at once inspired and dispirited by the distant sight of Chichester. He knew his way only by the talk he had had with one man or another, perhaps a messenger riding through, or a traveller at Lewes fair or the sheep market. Though he could move fairly easily a modest distance within his own country, and knew how to find his way along the London road that the Romans had laid down, his mind otherwise offered only names: beyond Chichester, Winchester; beyond Winchester, Salisbury; beyond Salisbury, Gloucester. And thereafter, Anne recalled, beyond the river's head, lay the far forest of Dean. Between these places seemed only emptiness and Harry had to keep his head down or he would have abandoned everything and gone creeping home.

'When you and Sir John were nigh to Chichester, where did you lodge? Was it within the city? It must be late when we get there tonight – the gates will be closed.'

'It was a place this side of Chichester. East – a little south, I reckon. There was a priory then – the guest house very clean and comfortable.'

'Well, we may at least shelter in the ruins,' Harry said. And he sent Colin on ahead to find out the way.

Colin was back in half an hour. 'The priory's all clutter and clobber, master – but the church still stand. There'd be shelter of a kind; but there's little other building and I see no place like to take us in.'

It was dusk when they reached the place. The fields came right up to the walls, and the hay lay raked and ready for cocking. Though the priory buildings were roofless, much of the walls still stood. Grass and weeds covered all the flooring; ivy the remnants of stairs and cloisters. Much stone had been quarried and taken away, and the round black ash-piles of travellers' fires seemed to be in every sheltering corner. The church, intact, was no doubt the parish church and saved because of it – though the parish offered very little more, it seemed, than the church farm, looking seedy and run-down, with a few dependent cottages. No window gaped in these, no door opened, as Dan drove the waggon in under the lee of a north wall, and the others followed.

Rest was not so easy that night. Anne was sure they would be roused and chased away as vagrants, or that some spirit out of the past might come to haunt them. It was in any case a haunted place, the sanctity gone out of it – the Garden of Eden itself must once have looked just so deserted by man. It distressed Anne bitterly, remembering how it had been when she came that way as a child.

'It saddens me like prayers for the dead, Harry.'

'And it should sadden your poor father, too, knowing you resting in such a manner here. But sleep easy. The dogs are keen – nothing shall slip by them, even though we all sleep fast.'

He watched her settle herself in the waggon, with Sukey and the children, while he and the two others stayed dozing by their fire. Every hour at the least, he rose and walked about the place to see that all was quiet. Each time he looked in at Anne and found her sleeping; but each time she woke enough to smile faintly, to hold out her hand to his; and each time it was as if she dropped some coin of comfort in his palm.

The short night was soon over. Morning came quiet and promising. Men appeared in the fields, but incurious, ignoring the travellers, beginning at once to rake the tossed hay into windrows. They were long used to comings and goings on this road, no doubt, and felt best to keep themselves to themselves, lest they were begged of, or threatened.

'This morning,' Anne said to Jack, 'we'll say our prayers in church.'

All went inside save Dan Morphew, who was left to guard the waggon and the horses and all the rest.

They went quietly into the tall church, which had a vaulted ceiling painted and fine, and there was already one worshipper ahead of them but no sign of a priest. The man was on his knees by the altar and murmuring and mumbling his prayers, so that his voice came to them like the drone of unnumbered swarming bees. He seemed not to hear them come in. He was wearing an old cowled robe with a girdle, and when he concluded his prayers and stood up, he pulled the robe over his head. He bundled it small, tied it with the girdle, and tucked it under his cloak as he turned up the nave.

He saw them as suddenly as if they had materialized before him out of air and light. He was a smallish man, his face much coarsened and sunburnt, but now his complexion changed to ashes. He came towards them in a hesitant manner, and when he was close enough, said in a voice that shook a little,

'Pray you, my children – never speak to any of my devotions here.'

Jack scuttled behind his mother in alarm, but Harry spoke kindly enough, saying they would be gone in an

hour, and knew none thereabouts to speak to of anything.

The man then asked in a stumbling way if they could spare him a crust of bread. This time it was Anne who answered.

The sun was already hot as they broke their fast together round the fire in the priory ruins.

'Do you travel far, sir?' the stranger asked Harry.

'Beyond the city of Gloucester,' Harry answered. Saying it proudly, he believed for the first time that so it would be; they would indeed ride in to Gloucester, they would ride beyond, they would reach their goal, however long it took, however wearily they came to it at the last.

'Then you travel first through great places,' the man said, 'where much is brought down and already half forgotten. But it shall build again – with God's help it shall build again.' He looked across the fire at Harry, frowning a little. 'Shall it not be so, my son?'

No one could answer this, but now they had recognized him for what he was, or had been.

'I was Brother Ambrose of this priory,' he told them, 'and we followed St Benedict. Here in this bundle is my monk's gown, that I put on each day as I say the office. Then it must be hid.' He smiled suddenly and was altogether transformed. 'I have made the pilgrimage many times from one shrine to another. To Salisbury ... To Gloucester ... For a little bread, should you wish it, I shall willingly guide you.'

As if repenting of the foul seasons that were past, the year now showed them another face. The summer lay over the south with all the neat beauty of a tapestry – bright blossom, dappled shade, with birds flying among silken trees, deer lightly running, small waterfalls to tinkle into haunted pools: it could have been a picture to some rhymed romance. The days were counted by their sunshine – Dan Morphew notched them on the cart's tailboard, and if there was haze, or cloud, or some modest shower, the notch was crossed at the bottom or at the top.

The disappearance of the monasteries offering hospitality to travellers no longer troubled them. Soon they gave up even the thought of sheltering indoors at night, making their camp rather in wooded places, or by some stream or riverside. Sleep under the open sky was light and easy. One man or another watched by the fire, the dogs beside him. The only alarms were sounds of animals that might be dangerous – boar, say, or horses running wild that could stampede their own. They killed and cooked, drank spring water, gathered in the early days wild strawberries and raspberries, begged cow's or goat's milk where they could, not always with success, but mostly so. Once Colin was chased away by a farmer's wife brandishing a great stick, and all her geese running ahead of her, far more terrifying than any woman. And once, passing through a wild and shabby village, where the church was in ruin and the manor house had gaping holes in the thatch and cattle in and out of the great hall, a crowd of boys ran after the travellers, throwing stones and making the sign against the evil eye. They shouted lewdly and sang out blasphemous rhymes, so that Anne called to Sukey to put her hands over Jack's ears.

Through these days, such as would always be remembered, Brother Ambrose led them sturdily, his strength returning as he came again to regular eating, his mind most excellently alert, his patience endless, his cooking best of all. Guide, cook and chaplain in one, he strode along the ancient roads in his battered old sandals and his shabby gown. Anne had stitched patches of coloured cloth on the inside, and so when he saw prudent, he dragged it off and wore it reversed. He taught Jack his letters and many prayers; he taught Dan Morphew to repeat the whole long Litany of the Saints, both in English and Latin – though this was less of an effort than it might have been in some instances; he spoke with Harry of the kings of England, the wars with France, the brutal conquest of the Scots. He liked to carry the baby, Lewis, against his shoulders, and jog him when he cried. At morning, at nightfall, he called them to their prayers, ending always with a supplication he had made up for himself: *Sweet Jesu, trampled and crucified, forgive us our times . . .*

In this way their journey became a wandering, without anxiety, without haste, yet never lacking purpose. Riding or walking, Anne moved at Harry's side, most often her hand in his. Nothing was said, no word of forgiveness, pardon, forgetting. Only as they were drawn back one to the other, their sorrows, which had been like a great heavy cloak over their shoulders, changed to a lighter covering, then to no more than a gossamery veil that the least wind might rend and scatter into unnoticed shreds.

Colin and Sukey laughed and quarrelled, the baby throve; Jack, burnt as a nut, dashed and shouted, and falling once into a deep pool with a dog almost on top of him, found that they both could swim. Thereafter he was in and out of every stream and pond and river that they came to, scaring away the otters that had already scared away the trout.

At night, when it was his turn to be on watch, Harry thought of what he had done, groaned that he had done it, cursed the harsh hard temper that had allowed him to leave as he had done, moving into another world unblessed, his memories of home clouded for ever by the manner of his leaving. Yet even here, alone and in the dark and truthful night, his anguish did ease. His father was a just man – he understood much – he would understand his eldest son and forgive him: Anne had said so . . .

The season mounted, the trees blew over-laden, the hedge roses bloomed and fell, elder flower and honeysuckle claimed the hedgerows, the bramble flowered, was spent, showed berries hard and green that might ripen with purple juices before the journey ended. In all this time, no danger threatened them worse than thunderstorms, no snakes were adders, no bee stung, no thief lurked.

'It seem to me heaven on earth,' said Anne.

'But hard times shall come again, surelye! We cannot have heaven for ever until we die!'

'It is heaven now!' she cried, laughing and leaning towards him.

It was the fresh forenoon of a day like many other, but it was the day on which, for the first time and it might be the last, he spoke of what had gone before they went to Mantlemass – of the lost child, the destruction of all they had known, the means by which they had been set upon the road, the long chain that dragged the past into the present as it must carry the present into the future.

'What if you and your father never rid this way before, never came by Staglye church at mass time – what then? What should have come to us both instead?'

'There should still be Ghylls Hatch,' Anne said. 'Best own to that . . . But there would no more be a Cecily Anne, my dear, than there is such a one now. So – eachway, anyway, she would be lost.'

They walked a long way in silence, but Anne's thought had not moved far in the time, for when she spoke again, she said, 'My beauteous daughter . . . I called her that before ever she were born. Do you recall, husband?'

'Aye.' And to make her smile, he recalled more, that harvest time when she was too far gone in pregnancy to take her share of the work, and how she had sat in the shade sulking while the rest toiled and laughed in the sun.

'But now,' he said, 'I have brought you to make your way among strangers. There shall be none you knew. I am all you have in the world.'

'I have Jack – I have Lewis. But they indeed are you.'

'I wonder can this be enough . . .'

'Aye,' she said. 'You've no cause to think otherly. Aye, my good love – so Judith call your father – aye, my good love, enough and plenty. And is it so wi' you?'

'It is,' he said . . .

When the summer went over, the fields standing in harvest, the nights chilled, the mornings freshened and the wandering came near its end. They rode through Gloucester out of a blackberry day, the gossamer taut over every spider's tent on every pinnacle of gorse. The streets of the city were fast and tumbling with people bound for market, returning from market. The babble of talk that rose between the buildings came after a long stretch of quiet and solitude, and so was all the more boisterous to the travellers. They, too, went to market, and later to that great church, to give thanks for the journey that was all but accomplished.

It was still early in the day. They quitted the city, and making better speed here, or else drawn on by anticipation, they turned down the gorge on the far side of the river. Ahead, the forest rose up over the steepness of the land, with here and there the first hints of gold on the beeches, the first touch of yellow on the bracken standing beneath. At that moment it was like coming home, though wisdom told them that not every forest could be the same. When they stopped at noon to eat and drink, they stopped for the last time – a man passing with a dog and two cows told them the direction in which Dame Furnival's manor lay. Then he said something more, but the words sounded too strange to be understood. Brother Ambrose, knowing perhaps strangely, more of the world and its diversities, reported what the man had said.

'He tells that the lady suffers much in her loneliness and widowhood; that she is robbed and put upon by her servants. You are her kin, I tell him. He says, She will rejoice to welcome any such.' He smiled at Harry. 'Divine Providence has brought you here, my son.'

They had paused to eat on a hillside, where the ground was open. Far below, they saw the river winding; far above them great birds wheeled.

'They are ravens,' Anne said. 'My uncle did name his house Ravenshall.'

When they had eaten and stamped out the fire, they looked about for Brother Ambrose, but he was not with them.

'Call him! Find him!' Harry cried, loud and commanding. 'He must be with us when we ride in!'

Though they called and searched and waited, he did not return. At last they knew that he was gone on his way. They might never see him again.

There seemed no more to stay them, yet Harry felt there must be more. He pulled out his knife and, kneeling struck it hard into the turf, which was cropped short and thick, and full of small flowering and creeping plants. The knife slid in, soft and easy, then struck and was held.

Harry peeled back the earth, carving it half a pace wide and broad, so that at last, beneath its cover, the stone showed, strong and challenging and familiar. He gazed down at it in silence. He might as well have been gazing on some soothsayer's magic mirror. He seemed to wince back from familiar fire and smoke and his ears filled with the hissing of molten metal, the swish of it through the bosh, the thud of the hammer as it cooled ...

He smiled at last and sat back on his heels. It seemed to him as if his bird of fire and smoke at that moment took wing and soared upward to where the ravens wheeled.

'See here, Dan,' he said. 'Here's why your cousins come to these parts from the Weald. The good stone, Dan – look, Colin, the streak of ore running in it. The iron, that shall make you both servant to a strong master.'

They had all clustered round. They made a small group in an untried land, but if any had doubts they were not shown. They looked all towards Harry. It was for him, now, to support them, and there would be no other Medley to call on, if things went wrong; no Mantlemass to offer shelter in any future trouble ...

Harry rose, saying it was time to go.

'Take Lewis, Sukey,' Anne said. 'The master and I shall ride on ahead. But take Jack up ahead of you, Harry. This day is for him, surelye. Whatever come later, Jack is your eldest.'

They mounted and moved off together, Anne a little ahead now since she was leading them to her kinsman's manor. They followed the rough track for no more than a mile. Then the trees stood back, the land parted into a wide, shallow valley. There at its head stood Ravenshall.

The Mantlemass Novels

What happier fate for any author than to live in a setting that demands to be written about?

This good fortune came my way when I made my home, a good many years ago, in a part of Sussex where several thousand acres remain of that great forest that once spread over all this countryside. I had known the place since childhood but only for walks and picnics. Suddenly, there it all was outside my garden gate, viewed from every window, ancient, mysterious and challenging.

I thought all the time of what I would one day write about the place. Long before I knew their names my characters were moving secretly through the forest, daring me to begin their story.

It took me ten years to pluck up courage and make a start. 'Cecily,' I wrote, 'had been brought to Mantlemass at dusk . . .'

What I certainly did not realize as I paused to consider that first line was that the last line would not be written for another twelve years.

B.W.

'It is true that one Mantlemass story grows out of what has gone before, and that the deepest satisfaction is reserved for those readers who read them all and in the right order ... Each novel, however, can be approached direct and enjoyed in isolation ...'
– Marcus Crouch, *The Times Literary Supplement*

The Lark and the Laurel – Wrenched from her idle and elegant life in London, Cecily Jolland is horrified to be left with her aunt at Mantlemass, buried deep in the Sussex forest. But unexpected freedom and her friendship with Lewis Mallory, help Cecily grow into a spirited young woman, and she learns that life at Mantlemass has much to offer her.

The Sprig of Broom – For Medley Plashet, son of a humble forest guide, life is full of riddles. What is the significance of the sprig of broom? What dark secret shrouds his father's past? Knowing his future happiness to be at stake, Medley is forced to seek out the truth.

A Cold Wind Blowing – Piers Medley's peaceful life is abruptly altered when his uncle is murdered before his eyes, leaving in his care a strange and silent young girl with no memory, it seems, of her former life. Drawn to her against his will, Piers is soon bewitched by Isabella. But despite the great happiness their love brings, Piers knows Isabella's past haunts her still.